The Exhaustive, Final,
Definitive, Last-Word,
No-Need-to-Search-Any-Further

# Guide to Surviving a Flawed System & Retiring with Confidence

by Wayne Fisher

# Contents

*"A goal without a plan
is just a wish."*

**Antoine de Saint-Exupery**

*(1900 - 1944)*

***

Dedicated to
Deborah S. Fisher

***

# Introduction

For over 26 years I have owned a financial services business in Northern California. I have focused on the needs of retired people and those soon to retire. Due to the last two market crashes, many of the people I get to visit with are seeking advice and shelter after losing a considerable portion of their life savings to **unprotected** stock market downturns.

Most people have a pretty good idea of what they want to do during retirement. The proper financing of this new journey is where the difficulty lies. The majority still have their life savings tied up in the Wall Street status quo: high-commission, low-performance funds. The same positions that failed them in the last two market crashes. They have no controls in place, no tactical plan, no safety net, no hedge, no stop-loss provision, no exit strategy and no tax considerations. What they do have is 100 percent excessive, unnecessary risk with a stark absence of planning.

Losing a significant portion of your retirement savings close to or during retirement is often a fatal blow to the plans you have made for your retired years. You simply cannot recover the lost savings—savings it took you most of your life to earn—in a short time period. The need for income from your savings further impedes the chance of recovery, since it's hard to replenish a pool of money that is now the source of your monthly income. It's like trying to fill a bucket with a hole in it.

But most retirees didn't know any other way.

The stock market has long been America's default method of retirement saving, its domination so unchallenged and enduring that Wall Street hasn't had to bother reselling itself to new generations or reinventing itself for changing times. That may not be your father's Oldsmobile, but this is his 401k. Retirement planning, or the lack of it, has remained virtually the same across generations. Had airplane manufacturers made as few advancements in air travel over the past 113 years of flight as Wall Street has made in retirement planning, the Boeing 787 Dreamliner would be made of sticks and cloth and would require hand starting.

Nobody keeps better statistics than Wall Street, so you might say they remember everything but have learned nothing.

Typical market-based investments owe their dominance as retirement-savings vehicles more to the American public's unawareness of alternatives than to a preponderance of happy outcomes. In fact, devastating economic reversals are common among those who play the market unprotected near or into retirement. People hit by such setbacks can no longer afford to pursue the plans they made for their golden years, nor realize the retirement lifestyle they once anticipated. Their futures are drastically altered, their stories desperate and sad. Wall Street ignores the more conservative, alternative investments; they just don't generate enough reoccurring revenue.

I hope writing about some of these stories as cautionary tales will do some good. Most people I meet with are insecure in their financial circumstances and frustrated with the ups and downs of their portfolios. They often respond to market downturns and crashes not by trading in the real source of their misery, but by bouncing from one broker to another. This does little good: they are just rebuying the same investment products under different-colored labels. And they are still taking direction from someone who is not licensed to give advice and whose business model does not include retirement planning. The financial tools and investments that retirees need are simply not in a broker-dealer's inventory. Putting a retiree's money in the broker's own proprietary funds solely because they pay higher commissions benefits whom? Recommending a fund because of bonus commissions (revenue sharing) is just how the business works. It's perfectly legal. It's just not very beneficial for the investor.

But today millions of people are jumping off Wall Street's greed-is-good rollercoaster in favor of practical, common sense investment alternatives, as well as new and better ways to help protect their securities-based (stock-based) investments. They can now enjoy their retirement years. If you've jumped off, good for you. And if you haven't yet, this book is for you. Its pages are full of heartache, yes, but also full of hope.

There are better ways to manage your retirement savings and income. My goal is to help you find *your* way.

I won't kid you. Nothing in this book is top secret. But much of the information and direction you'll find here isn't easy to come by in the financial-services industry. Why are most retirement savings still being invested in the very products that failed in the last two market crashes? Because it is very profitable for the sellers—just not very beneficial for the consumer. And most people simply don't know about the alternatives to this flawed system. So, what does a good alternative to Wall Street look like? Just this: the choice of investment vehicles and financial tools that have weathered the storms, protected principal and produced reasonable gains, all while leveraging a sustainable income. The proper choice for you should take into consideration your circumstances, goals and timeline, plus a planning and saving method that considers every aspect of yourself and your needs—all integrated into a flexible, comprehensive retirement game plan.

Why have so few retirees been shown what you are about to learn? Because *licensed* advisors, who are indeed licensed to provide financial *advice* and alternatives, are few and far between.

As you get older, the game changes. You need to eliminate the gambling feature at the heart of your retirement investments. You must get this right the first time—unless you think this retirement is only a practice run for your next retirement.

I left the broker-dealer world a long time ago because it didn't offer what my clients needed. Wall Street is a flawed system driven by chance and luck, all at a very high price tag. The cycle changes with the wind and, bam, that's the end of people's dreams. There goes the Winnebago, and here comes a reverse mortgage.

Having a solid, well thought-out *game plan* gives you control and peace of mind. You don't have to be a financial victim. You can be an economic survivor, and you can indeed survive this flawed system and retire with confidence.

## Notes

(1) An effort has been made to share this information in a simple manner with a minimum industry jargon. I have included a few of my experiences and observations, with both old and new life lessons.

(2) The term *investment* applies to financial products where principal is at risk. Financial products where principal is protected I will refer to as *financial tools*.

(3) The Standard and Poor's 500 (S&P 500) is the most widely used *benchmark* for measuring overall market performance and condition. It represents more than 80% of market activity. Bear in mind its value as you consider this material.

## Financial Disclosure and Disclaimer

- Investment Adviser Representative of/and investment advisory services offered through Royal Fund Management, LLC. Royal Fund Management is registered as an investment adviser with the SEC and only transacts business in states where it is properly registered, or is excluded or exempted from registration requirements. SEC registration does not constitute an endorsement of the firm by the Commission nor does it indicate that the adviser has attained a particular level of skill or ability.

- Information presented is believed to be factual and up-to-date, but we do not guarantee its accuracy and it should not be regarded as a complete analysis of the subjects discussed. All expressions of opinion reflect the judgment of the author as of the date of publication and are subject to change. Content should not be construed as personalized investment advice nor should it be interpreted as an offer to buy or sell any securities mentioned. A professional advisor should be consulted before implementing any of the strategies presented.

- Past performance may not be indicative of future results. All investment strategies have the potential for profit or loss. Different types of investments involve varying degrees of risk, and there can be no assurance that any specific investment or strategy will be suitable or profitable for an investor.

- The tax, legal, and estate planning information provided is general in nature. It should not be construed as legal or tax advice. Always consult an attorney or tax professional regarding your specific legal or tax situation.

- Historical performance results for investment indexes and/or categories generally do not reflect the deduction of transaction and/or custodial charges or the deduction of an investment-management fee, the incurrence of which would have the effect of decreasing historical performance results. There are no assurances that an investor's portfolio will match or outperform any particular benchmark.

# Chapter 1: Camped on the Edge

## Coping with Risk

Risk is inherent to life. If you are alive, you are *at risk* of injury and death. It is something we have always had to deal with from our earliest memories. We live and we learn. Countless lessons of what not to do again have been filed away under our mental *trial and error* tab. (For instance, sticking one of mom's bobby pins into a wall socket.) To protect us all, there are ongoing improvements to safeguards: better training wheels, brakes, seat belts, helmets, guard rails and the like. All these are intended to keep us safe and manage the risks we encounter.

You have probably applied risk management to protect yourself and your family in every area of your life except one. You have failed to safeguard your retirement savings and the stream of income you will depend on after your monthly paycheck stops. After leaving your life's work, *growing your savings* is your new job, and your salary is the stream of income that it will generate. If you have not connected the dots between the volatility pointed at your retirement savings and the risk to your future monthly income, this would be a really good time to find a pencil.

## Risk Management and Common Sense

I started my working life as a risk manager, an underwriter for a property-casualty insurance company. Later I worked for and managed a retail business insurance agency that provided commercial insurance in five states. When you are protecting the physical assets and liability exposures for a business owner, you should be looking for the worst-case scenarios. Consider all the "what if" situations and use them as a prevention checklist for the planning process. This exercise most certainly needs to be applied to your retirement savings.

## We All Live in Harm's Way

I can see two volcanoes from my home in rural Northern California. Mt. Lassen stands 38 miles to the East at an elevation of 10,463 feet. It is considered active, though the last notable eruption was in May of 1915 and it has been relatively quiet since 1917. Mt. Shasta, 57 miles to the North, is

14,180 feet in elevation. Considered potentially active, it last erupted in 1786. Evidence of the destructive power of these two mountains is found throughout our area—reminders of their potential for changing the landscape. My home is built on a boulder pile said to have come from one of Mt. Lassen's ancient blasts. The boulders are even part of the home's foundation. You might say I live at risk, camped on the edge of destruction—*along with tens of thousands of others*. Moreover, my house is camped on the edge of a gorge. The property drops off abruptly, heading down to a creek 150 feet below. Much of that distance is a straight vertical drop, and some is even under-cut. (Though there is a trail leading down to the creek if you know where to find it.)

Why would someone live in an area with such permanent potential for a flying-boulder, hot-ash rainstorm? Because common sense and a little risk management tells us this is an acceptable risk.

- (1) Analysis: It has been a long time since either volcano has erupted. With modern equipment, volcanologists do a good job of warning us, long in advance, of pending eruptions. Everybody had been warned about Mt. Saint Helens; some chose not to leave.

- (2) Comparison: I lived on the Texas–Arkansas border for 25 years. I have seen the effects of tornados that drop out of the sky without warning and suck up 200-hundred-year-old oak trees, even ripping up blacktop paving from highways. I prefer the volcanoes.

- (3) Mitigating Hazards: Should the volcano erupt and boulders rain down from the sky, I know where the caves are located along the creek at the bottom of the gorge. It would be foolish to seek shelter in my house—but the caves would provide solid limestone protection, 150 feet thick.

What about you—are you living with acceptable risk? How vulnerable are you to a market reversal caused by some newsworthy event? Could your savings suddenly be less than you need to support your lifestyle?

Do you know how to find a safe place?

Most people don't realize their retirement savings and the monthly income it generates are at such risk of loss until it's too late. I can't begin to relate how many times people have told me, "I am not worried about my savings. My broker has me completely out of the stock market—I am 100% in mutual funds." They had no clue their life savings were in such a volatile position.

They were just like Hannah on the zip line.

My youngest granddaughter Hannah was first in line for the fourth zip line run during a family excursion into the mountains just south of Puerto Vallarta, Mexico. We had to crawl up a mountain and climb a tower to reach this zip line. The cable stretched out across a gorge and then *through a tunnel.*

Hannah began her ride squealing with delight as she crossed the open area 75 feet above the jungle, twisting from side to side and kicking her feet as if to say, "Go faster, faster!" Then she disappeared into the darkness of the tunnel.

I was next with a completely different style: legs straight out, toes pointed, elbows tucked in. I wanted to enter that tunnel straight as an arrow to avoid crashing into the jagged sides. From the tower, the opening looked to be about the size of a VW Bug. As I approached the entrance, I could barely see because my eyes were watering so much from the wind. But the closer look told me the opening was about the size of a bus—maybe two buses.

When I joined her at the landing area, Hannah grabbed my hand and pulled me toward the next zip line. The reason she was so bold and eager for this new adventure, without pause or reservation, came to me right there: she was only seven. Hannah had not lived long enough to understand potential dangers, the consequences of falling, nor just how severely injured you can become if things go awry. She was simply "inexperienced."

I looked at the situation differently. Like most adults, I completely understood the consequences. Between horses, motorcycles and football I have broken a few body parts and experienced the associated pain.

Many of the people I meet with share Hannah's inexperience in their financial lives. As they have aged, they have still not realized that they need to adopt a new and more cautious paradigm.

Here are a few examples of couples who were unaware of the volatility pointed at their retirement savings. They failed to manage their risk.

## Lessons in Failure

For all practical purposes, these five couples beat the system. They won. All had grown their savings to an enviable retirement nest egg of around $500,000. The biggest contributor to their financial success was **timing**, also called *sequence of events* (which I will illustrate later). They just so happened to land on a very positive economic trend. The gains to their retirement savings were pushed along by one of the greatest secular bull market trends in history. I'm sharing these couples' stories because of the severity of their losses. This could happen to you too. They would all tell you: they never expected it to happen to them.

These are real people. They are intelligent and skillful in their various fields of endeavor. But when it came to their retirement savings, they relied on the wrong business model to handle their money.

(1) Bob and Karen raised four children in the San Francisco Bay Area.[1] With no pensions in view, they strove to save money in Bob's 401(k). Exceptionally successful, they saved over $500,000 for retirement. Like many Bay Area residents, they also cashed in on the high equity value in their home, moved to rural Northern California, purchased a home and acreage for cash, and prepared to travel and enjoy their retirement years. They rolled over the 401(k) into an IRA with a local branch office for a national broker-dealer. And then they watched as their life savings slowly melted down. Their broker repeatedly encouraged them to "hold on; it will come back." A relative referred them to me. When we met, only $173,000 of their $500,000 nest egg remained.

---

[1] All client names in this book are invented. The people described here are real but their names have been changed to protect their privacy.

We developed a plan to deliver enough income now, while deferring a portion of their savings to a second position. That position grew into a lifetime stream of money beyond the reach of Wall Street. Now with a reverse mortgage on the property they had hoped to leave their children, Bob and Karen are still enjoying their retirement—though perhaps not as much as they could have.

Did I hear someone say, "It's only a paper loss until you sell"? Ah. You see, Bob and Karen were in their early 70s. For years they had anticipated traveling the United States and Canada in their RV—which requires money. Their plan never included sitting on their porch for 5–10 years while their losses were replaced with new gains. That is, if they didn't suffer further losses.

(2) Betty heard my radio program and asked her husband to contact me for an appointment. I visited with her husband, and he liked what I showed him. Later, he and Betty came in together for further details. She commented, "When I married Joe* six years ago he had over $500,000 in his IRA. ... Every time the value goes down," he "freezes up." Such paralysis is not uncommon with people who don't

know what else to do. The value of Joe's IRA had dropped to $86,000. Nearing age seventy, Joe was still working. In her mid-sixties, Betty was providing day care for small children in their home. Now that $86,000 is growing with market-based gains, but out of the reach of Wall Street.

(3) A friend's referral brought in Jim and Joanne. He had worked in tech sales, she for the phone company. They had a combined net savings of just over $500,000 in their brokerage account, which included his IRA, their discretionary savings, and what had been her company pension (now invested as an IRA, since her employer bought out her pension for $178,000 cash). When I met with them, they had less than $40,000 left and wanted to know if I had any hot stock tips. They were in their late sixties, so I suggested they stay away from hot stocks and put their remaining funds in their credit union.

(4) Gene came in for a consultation in early 2007. He had been a disciplined saver, efficient with his spending—even paying off his home mortgage in his thirties. He explained with pride how he had almost recovered his losses from the 2000-2002

market crash: he had almost broken even with his original $486,000. He had spent nearly eight years feverishly working to make new gains and rebuild what he had lost, taking a lot of risks in the process. Now that he was retired, I suggested two conservative positions which would give him market-based gains and a *pension-like*, lifetime income—without ever exposing his principal to another market meltdown. But he told me that he and his broker had it all laid out. The market was going to soar for the next several years, and he was going to benefit *big time* from all this prosperity. Then came 2008 and the failure of his prosperity. The last I heard his holdings were below $200,000.

(5) Frank and Ginger came in one day in 2009; they had had a previous appointment with me about a year and a half earlier. I said, "Great to see you again. What brings you back in?" Frank answered, "$226,000." That was what not changing to a conservative position and staying in the market during 2008 cost them. But now their savings is growing, ready to pay them a lifetime stream of income whenever they need it.

These failures have a common cause.

In all of them, people relied on a flawed system to manage their retirement savings. They all put their money and their trust into the hands of brokers not licensed to give financial advice,[2] licensed only to sell the investments in the inventory of their broker-dealer employer.

There was no provision for retirement planning, nor for risk reduction as they aged. And when the losses started to occur, the only advice that offered to them was *"Hang in there, it'll come back!"*

---

[2] The term *advisor* is the most misused and misleading word in the financial services industry. Very few individuals selling investments and financial tools are licensed advisors. An article titled "A Modest Proposal: Prosecute Non-Fiduciaries Using Term 'Advisor'" explains: "'If someone would like to seek advice on a specific financial product, or about their own overall situation, they should get it from a financial advisor working to the fiduciary standard who is familiar with their financial situation,' says Helaine Olen, author of a new book blasting the personal finance industry, called *Pound Foolish*. 'I've seen way too many people hurt financially as a result of taking the counsel of salesmen promoting various financial products who don't have a legal responsibility to act in their customers' best interests,' Olen told AdvisorOne." (Gil Weinreich, *AdvisorOne*. April 8, 2013.)

## These Words Have Cost Retirees Untold Savings and Misery

In the history of investing, money has rarely ever come back. Those are words of consolation for widows and orphans—attempts to diminish the severity of their losses and their pain. Money has serial numbers, which makes it easy to identify should it ever return to your account. But *"Hang in there, it'll come back"* sounds so much better than the truth. The truth sounds like this: "Okay, now you have lost that money. It's gone. But if you leave what's left of your life savings right where it's at, should the economic winds change direction you might make some gains this time—or you might continue to lose."

If you have accumulated a surplus of money and one of your stocks just took a dramatic drop, you should not sell at the bottom unless you have a good reason. If, however, you need all your money to finance your retirement, then don't gamble with it.

All the money in the stories above was retirement savings, and every dollar of it was needed.

What you've got is all you have. Doctors, grocery stores and gas stations don't accept promissory notes or IOUs. If you need medical care, food or fuel, you must pay for it upon delivery.

The older we get, the more we should remember the old saying: "It's not what you make that matters; it's what you keep." Better to get the return OF your principal than a prospect of return ON your principal.

Saving what you have now has taken most of your life. Common sense should tell you that if you lose your savings now, you do not have enough *life* left to replace them.

*"Everybody has a plan until they get punched in the mouth."*

***Mike Tyson***

# Chapter 2: Surviving a Flawed System

The stock market (and most of those invested in it) have suffered through two major crashes since 2000. From 2000 to 2002 the S&P 500® lost 50% of its value, and in 2008 it lost another 37%. The very same investment products that failed have been resold to these investors and then resold again, without improvement. Most of the people I meet with have very little understanding of how their investments work and what they pay in fees. Nor do they imagine that there is a separate universe of conservative opportunities out there, opportunities that could have protected their principal while delivering reasonable market-based gains! Continuing to use Wall Street's favorite funds will not fare any better in the next crash. Albert Einstein best described this approach to experimentation as, "*Insanity*: Doing the same thing over and over again and expecting different results."

In the following chapters, we will explore some of the shortcomings of this flawed system which has caused retirees so much grief. Thankfully, we will also examine the available solutions.

The following report first aired as the dust was settling on the market crash of 2008.

> "The effects of the current economic crisis have touched everyone. Even if you still have a good job and a paid-up mortgage, chances are your monthly 401(k) statement will remind you that you've lost a good chunk of your savings.[3]
>
> Trillions of dollars have evaporated from those accounts that have become the prime source of retirement funds for a majority of American workers, affecting their psyche and their future. If you are still young enough, there's time to rebuild and recover, but if you are in your 50s, 60s or beyond the consequences can be dire, **and it's drawing attention to the shortcomings of a retirement system that**

---

[3] The Wall Street funds offered in 401(k)s are similar in kind and quality of those offered in all other investments.

**has jeopardized the financial security of tens of millions of people."[4]**

A considerable portion of those lost savings came from new contributions and gains added to accounts over the previous eight years, as workers were still trying to recover from the losses of the 2000-2002 market crash.

Here's another report about 401(k)s.

**"Rep. Miller pegs 401(k)s as high stakes crap shoot**

> In the first of a series of hearings exploring the shortcomings of the nation's retirement system, House Education and Labor Committee Chairman Rep. George Miller, D-Calif., referred to America's 401(k) plans as little more than a 'high stakes crap shoot,' citing deep flaws have existed in the nation's retirement system even when the market was performing well.

---

[4] CBS 60 Minutes: *Older Americans' 401(k)s Have Plummeted; Many Fear They Will Never Get To Retire.* April 17, 2009. You can watch the original video at https://www.youtube.com/watch?v=nAHgr9dY9BU.

> 'We are realizing that Wall Street's guarantees of predictable benefits and peace of mind throughout retirement was nothing more than a hallow promise,' Miller said in his opening statement. 'While 401(k)s are a fact of life, this committee has found that these plans in their current form do not and will not provide sufficient retirement security for the vast majority of Americans. That is why in the short term, we must preserve and strengthen 401(k)s. Hidden fees and conflicts of interest must be rooted out. And, 401(k)s need to be run in the interest of account holders, not the financial services industry.'"[5]

## Is the Market Efficient?

Now there's a question that will divide the room. Simply put, *market efficiency* or the *degree of efficiency* is the value of the performance you should expect from your money when invested in the stock market, and what needs to be done on your part to

---

[5] ThinkAdvisor, February 24, 2009. http://www.thinkadvisor.com/2009/02/24/rep-miller-pegs-401ks-as-high-stakes-crap-shoot

receive the maximum benefit. Half of the room says you must be proactive; the other half says you can sleep through it and do just as well.

Let's not argue. Let's engage common sense and do some math in four areas not usually considered.

## (1) Understanding the True Impact of Losses

First, you need to recognize that losses are much more critical to your retirement savings than you think. Losses and gains are not equal in the way they impact your savings: Dollars gained do not replace dollars lost. When a loss occurs (large or small) the power you once held in leveraging new gains from your savings has been reduced. Your *basis* has been reduced. When the market "breaks even" your money does not.

For example, say you had $100,000 invested in the market before its 50% downturn in the dot-com crash of 2000-2002. If you fared as well as the S&P 500, you would have $50,000 remaining in 2002. After the S&P 500 accumulates another 50% in growth, it is back up to "break even." But after you have captured 50% growth, your new total is just $75,000—because you built back on a reduced basis of only $50,000. This 50% gain may come from capital appreciation, dividends or magic beans; it doesn't matter. You're still down $25,000 on your money.

Granted, this illustration shows a severe drop in value because it was driven by a major market crash. But the yo-yo effect of daily ups and downs of the market can be just as damaging—it's merely harder to identify the cumulative effect of smaller sums. This isn't the new math or the old math; it is simply the *aftermath*. Remember: In the market, you need a 100% gain to recover from a 50% loss. Protect your principal.

## (2) The High Cost of the Status Quo

The net *cost* of a Wall Street fund has been compared to an iceberg. Only a small portion is visible from the surface—a larger portion is often hidden. You need to be wary of excessively high *costs* (like fees, commissions and expenses). These can eat away at your savings like a cancer. For example, more than 50% of what you deposit into mutual funds will over time go to fees, commissions and expenses. The type of tax qualification (where the funds are held) doesn't really matter: IRA, Roth, 401k, 403B, 457, TSP or your discretionary savings.

*"The cancer to your retirement savings is mutual fund fees. Over time, 54% of your money will go to fees."*

***Clark Howard, CNN HLN News***
*Friday, April 23, 2010*

Fees, fees, and more fees! Fees reported as $404 per year were discovered to actually be $14,552 per year. The effect: reducing retirement benefits by 40% to 60%. A fee of 2% can devour 50% of your retirement savings over time.[6]

A small fee can be very costly over time. An extra 1.5% in hidden annual *costs* robbed this retiree of $180,129.

---

[6] "Bloomberg 401k fee discussion" on YouTube. www.youtube.com/watch?v=dqCilKVKla0. Watch this three-part series of videos.

| | | |
|---|---|---|
| Beginning Value: | $250,000 | $250,000 |
| Growth Over Time: | 5% / year | 5% / year |
| Time Period: | 25 years | 25 years |
| Total Annual Costs: | -2.5% | -1% |
| Ending Value: | $666,459 | $846,459 |

Determine your total annual *costs* from an independent, third-party source. Beware of excessive *fees, commissions* and *expenses*.

Beyond the usual costs, mutual fund companies pay incentive bonuses to brokers for placing client money with them. It's called *revenue sharing*. These bonuses are commonplace—but is there a chance your broker is recommending funds for the sake of his wallet, not yours? Could another investment (perhaps one chosen for its characteristics) be more beneficial for you? If you can't locate the "Revenue Sharing Disclosure" information in your statement, request a copy.

And then there are *proprietary* mutual funds. These are built by a broker-dealer to be sold only by their employees. For the most part, these funds are created to be sold, not bought.

I had handled most of Barry's* savings for several years when he finally retired from his dental practice. He brought his 401k statement to my office to roll it to an IRA. He commented, "I don't have the money here that I paid into this thing. It certainly has never made any money for me." When I opened the statement, I saw three pages of mutual funds listed. The name of each mutual fund began with the name of his 401k company, one of the largest providers of 401Ks. These were all proprietary mutual funds: high in commissions, low in performance. (Some broker-dealers use another name for their proprietary mutual funds to make it less transparent.)

Some people are fighting back against expensive proprietary funds:

> "A lawsuit brought by a group of current and former employees of financial services firm Ameriprise has been allowed to proceed. The suit alleges that Ameriprise violated their

fiduciary obligations as the sponsor of the 401(k) plan it offers to employees. The main issue is that Ameriprise offered a number of its proprietary mutual funds as options in the plan; these funds were allegedly expensive compared to other non-proprietary options that could have been utilized. Further it is alleged that these funds paid revenue sharing and other fees to Ameriprise and several of its subsidiaries. The implications of this suit are pretty clear. If Ameriprise is found to be guilty of breaching its Fiduciary duty by stocking their 401(k) plan with sub-par, expensive proprietary funds this moves us further along the path of accountability by retirement plan sponsors for the retirement plans offered to their employees in my opinion."

***The Chicago Financial Planner*, February 13, 2013, by Roger Wohlner.**

The results?

"Ameriprise to pay $27.5 million settlement in 401(k) fiduciary breach suit: Firm denies allegations made by its own retirement plan participants"[7]

These more expensive proprietary funds and the practice of revenue sharing is commonplace among the broker-dealer world.

Don't accept sub-par funds. You need a compelling reason to put your hard-earned money into any investment. Knowing the total *costs* and how an investment will benefit you is crucial. Before you place your money in an "at-risk" investment, use third-party information to help you decide.

## Stop Paying Fees on Money That's Not Yours

Are you paying fees, commissions and expenses on Uncle Sam's money? If you have a pre-tax savings account (IRA, 401K, etc.) it's not all your money—you have a partner. You share ownership with the tax man, and you are paying fees on money that

---

7 Article by Darla Mercado, accessible at http://www.investmentnews.com/article/20150326/FREE/150329942/ameriprise-to-pay-27-5-million-settlement-in-401-k-fiduciary-breach. Mar 26, 2015.

you will eventually pay in taxes. To make matters worse, when you turn 70 ½ you must begin taking your RMDs (Required Minimum Distributions). The percentage of these distributions increases every year, with the effect of making you spend down all this money during your lifetime. There are painless strategies to get your pre-tax money to an after-tax position. It is best not to share ownership of your money.

Where does all this money go?

> "While government prosecutors pursue lawsuits against JPMorgan and Wells Fargo for 'misconduct' in the mortgage market and Wall Street firms complain about new regulations, compensation on the Street is rising.
>
> New York State Comptroller Thomas DiNapoli reports that total compensation at Wall Street firms rose 4% last year to more than $60 billion—near pre-crash levels—and the third highest level ever.
>
> This is an astounding chunk of change, $60 billion, says The Daily Ticker's Henry Blodget.

> It represents nearly half of all revenue earned by Wall Street.
>
> The average pay package of financial industry employees in New York State was $362,950 in 2011, more than seven times the national median household income of just over $50,000, which often reflects the pay of two working adults."[8]

Does your broker continue charging you fees while your account is losing value? You may want to consider a new strategy.

## (3) The Failure of Wall Street's Diversification

We have all been forever warned not to put all our eggs in one basket, because should we trip on the way back from the chicken house, there will be no breakfast. We are advised to use multiple baskets or make more than one trip. There you have it: spread of risk or diversification.

---

[8] The Daily Ticker / Yahoo Financial / October 11, 2012

The purpose of a mutual fund is to provide instant diversification, which seems to satisfy the concerns of not putting all your eggs in one basket. The Dutch are credited with developing mutual funds. They began using them in 1774, and the whole idea was to *diversify*—to spread out the chance of loss or to lower the severity of a loss. So instead of putting all your money in one stock you can now drop your money into a box of 25 stocks and have an instant spread of risk. This is logical. It sounds good too. But history gives us a clearer understanding: Mutual funds do well only when the stocks in them do well. And in the last two market crashes, Wall Street's version of diversification through mutual funds generally failed to deliver.

Let's compare your mutual funds with the S&P 500 Composite Index. This is an equity index which includes 500 of America's best, strongest and wealthiest companies. They are large cap, they are blue chip, and this index has been keeping score since 1926. It is the epitome of diversification, including companies from Caterpillar Equipment to Microsoft, from Coca-Cola to Home Depot, from Campbell Soup to Raytheon.

If you think the diversification inside your mutual fund offers safety through its spread-of-risk strategy, consider the history of the S&P 500. Compared to the 25 or so stocks in your mutual fund, the S&P 500 is 20 times more diversified. Still, it lost 50% of its value between 2000 and 2002, and lost 37% in 2008. No wonder your mutual funds did so poorly.

By the way, did you know that the S&P 500 outperforms 80% to 90% of mutual funds, year in and year out? Keep that in mind as we go along. There are strategies providing indexed-based gains along with principal protection.

Here's a question for the skeptics: Did most mutual fund investors lose money in the last two market crashes? They did. So what happened to the benefits of diversification with mutual funds? Most mutual funds are not a good delivery system for the *functioning diversification* that retirees need.

## The New Diversification: Open Your Eyes to Alternatives

Periods of high volatility produce correlation among investments. The market runs as a herd—all in the same direction. Diversification is non-correlation. The chart on the following page compares undiversified (correlated) and diversified (non-correlated) portfolios. During both market downturns, diversification provided no protection for a retiree's life savings.

TRADITIONAL DIVERSIFICATION CAN BE LACKING WHEN VOLATILITY RISES

"Undiversified" vs. "Diversified" Portfolio Performance

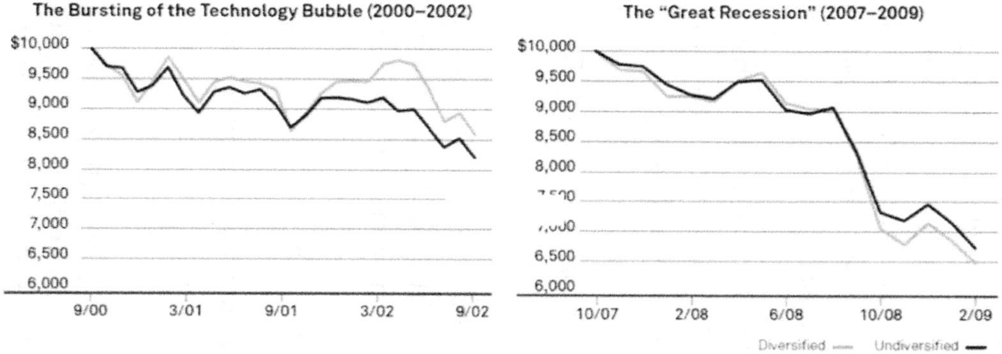


Sources: BlackRock; Informa Investment Solutions. Past performance is no guarantee of future results. The information provided is for illustrative purposes only and is not meant to represent the performance of any particular investment. The data assumes reinvestment of all income and does not account for taxes or transaction costs. It is not possible to invest directly in an index. **Undiversified Portfolio** is composed of 60% S&P 500 Index and 40% Barclays Credit Index. **Diversified Portfolio** is composed of 12% S&P 500 Index, 12% S&P 400 Mid Cap Index, 12% S&P 600 Small Cap Index, 12% MSCI EAFE Index, 12% MSCI Emerging Markets Index, 13.3% Barclays Credit Index, 13.3% Barclays US Treasury Index and 13.3% Barclays Capital US High Yield Index. The time frame used for "The Bursting of the Technology Bubble (2000-2002)" is September 1, 2000 through September 30, 2002. The time frame used for "The 'Great Recession' (2007-2009)" is November 1, 2007 through February 28, 2009.

Dr. Christopher Geczy says, "The notion of 'alternative' investing is often misunderstood. Gaining access to different types of investments is an approach that almost everyone should employ, and many strategies are now available to a broad range of individuals."[9]

Retirees do need to reduce their risk of capital loss as they age. But there are better ways of providing *real* and *efficient* diversification.

## Risk Management Through Risk Reduction

I recall the study material for my (SEC) Series 65 license making the point that you cannot diversify inside the stock market. For real diversification, you need to reposition a growing portion of your savings outside the market as you age.

Imagine an island surrounded by ships loaded with gold and precious stones. Some ships were

---

[9] Dr. Christopher Geczy, "The New Diversification Open Your Eyes to Alternatives." Alternatives Investment Education Center: Tools: Financial Professionals: Blackrock. Web. 29 March 2014.

constructed of wood, some of steel, and others of the latest carbon fiber blends—but when a great storm blew in they all sank. The wise captain who knew storms were common to this area saved his cargo. How? By moving it from his ship to a stone fortress at the top of the island.

If having enough monthly income during retirement is of genuine concern to you, you must reduce the volatility pointed at your pool of money. As you age, you need to reposition more of your savings to places offering *principal protection*. Reducing risk does not mean putting your money on a shelf—you still need to have growth on your savings, and you certainly can.

## (4) Sequence of Events

Some people can choose when they retire; others cannot. But the condition of the market and how it can impact your hard-earned savings is entirely out of your control. The two events that will eventually converge are (1) when you retire and (2) the market conditions just before and during your retirement.

Here is how the *Sequence of Events* can impact the rest of your life.

(A) The **Annual Return** column on the following illustration shows how gains and losses accumulate.

(B) The **Inverse Return** column reverses the order of gains and losses, and we end up with the same value.

But look at the second illustration. Notice how things change when you retire and start to withdraw an annual income of $35,000 (increased for inflation) to help finance your retirement.

## Accumulation on $500,000 Inverse Returns Effect

| Year | Annual Return | End of Year Value | Inverse Return | End of Year Value |
|---|---|---|---|---|
| 1 | +28% | $640,000 | -38% | $310,000 |
| 2 | -10% | $576,000 | -12% | $272,800 |
| 3 | +15% | $662,400 | +2% | $278,256 |
| 4 | +17% | $775,008 | +15% | $319,994 |
| 5 | +1% | $782,758 | +26% | $403,193 |
| 6 | +26% | $986,275 | +1% | $407,225 |
| 7 | +15% | $1,134,216 | +17% | $476,453 |
| 8 | +2% | $1,156,901 | +15% | $547,921 |
| 9 | -12% | $1,018,073 | -10% | $493,129 |
| 10 | -38% | A **$631,205** | +28% | B **$631,205** |

(A) The ANNUAL RETURN end of year value column shows how gains and losses accumulated.

(B) The INVERSE RETURN end of year column reverses the order of gains and losses and we end up with the same value.

## Income on $500,000 Inverse Returns Effect

| Year | Annual Return | Annual Withdraw | End of Year Value | Inverse Return | End of Year Value |
|---|---|---|---|---|---|
| 1 | +28% | $35,000 | $605,000 | -38% | $275,000 |
| 2 | -10% | $36,050 | $508,450 | -12% | $205,950 |
| 3 | +15% | $37,132 | $547,586 | +2% | $172,938 |
| 4 | +17% | $38,245 | $602,430 | +15% | $160,633 |
| 5 | +1% | $39,393 | $569,062 | +26% | $163,004 |
| 6 | +26% | $40,575 | $676,443 | +1% | $124,060 |
| 7 | +15% | $41,792 | $736,118 | +17% | $103,358 |
| 8 | +2% | $43,046 | $707,795 | +15% | $75,816 |
| 9 | -12% | $44,337 | $578,522 | -10% | $23,898 |
| 10 | -38% | $45,667 | **A** **$313,017** | +28% | **B** **(-$15,078)** |

Now compare (A) and (B). Notice how the end of year values change when you retire and start drawing an annual income of $35,000 to help finance your retirement; this scenario has been adjusted for inflation.

Notice the differences at year 10 on the two **End of Year Value** columns above. This illustrates the impact of the **Sequence of Events**: where your retirement savings converge with current market conditions. And it is a coin toss.

If your savings is at full risk, you have no control on how the market will impact your pool of money and your monthly income. When you encounter risk, chance and timing, you need to become more conservative with your money, seeking out investments and alternative financial tools which provide principal protection.

Again, reducing risk does not mean giving up gains. Consider the chart on the following page. *Account A* consists of Wall Street funds, while *Account B* is made up of conservative and principal-protected investments. Which account would you rather own?

| | Account A = $100,000 | Account B = $100,000 |
|---|---|---|
| Year 1 | +14.00% | +4.75% |
| Year 2 | +16.00% | +4.75% |
| Year 3 | +7.00% | +4.75% |
| Year 4 | -9.00% | +4.75% |
| Year 5 | +5.00% | +4.75% |
| Year 6 | -12.00% | +4.75% |
| Year 7 | +9.00 | +4.75% |
| Year 8 | -3.00% | +4.75% |
| Year 9 | +13.00% | +4.75% |
| Year 10 | +10.00% | +4.75% |
| TOTAL | **$156,361** | **$156,361** |

**Who was more content, slept better and was able to cope with daily life and family? The owner of Account A or B?**

**"Among respondents with relationship stress aged 44 to 54; 44% said money was the primary cause."** *Fighting with Your Spouse? It's probably about this.* **CNBC Personal Finance; Kelly Holland. February 4, 2015**

## The Last 118 Years of the Dow: 60% Bear and 40% Bull

Now let's take a history lesson from the Dow Jones Industrial Average® and see how the convergence of these two events (*when you retire* and *market conditions*) might impact your retirement savings and income.

The chart on the next page shows that the Dow Jones Industrial Average can experience long, drawn-out bull and bear market secular trends. The gains and losses shown are cumulative for the years illustrated. In rounded numbers, 60% of the last 118 years were spent in bear market secular trends, 40% in bull market secular trends.

Similar trends run throughout market history. They are controlled by the level of comfort of those who are trading in the market. Today, that level of comfort may be impacted by not only domestic newsworthy events but also worldwide events. Enthusiasm can quickly turn pessimistic.

*"Those who don't know history are*
*doomed to repeat it."*
***Edmund Burke***

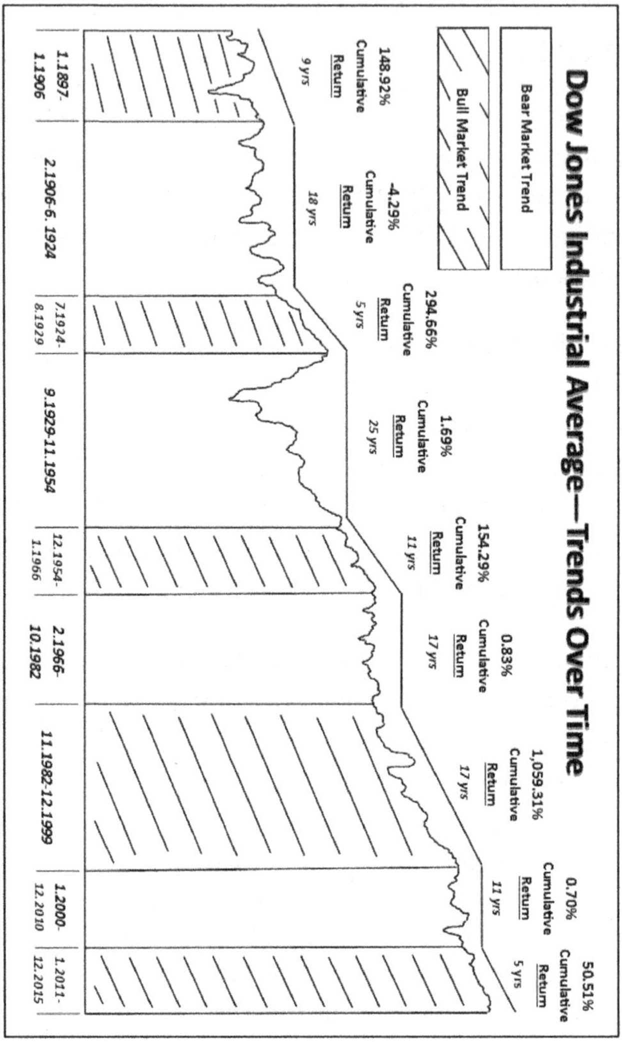
Dow Jones Industrial Average—Trends Over Time
Bear Market Trend
Bull Market Trend
148.92% Cumulative Return
9 yrs
-4.29% Cumulative Return
18 yrs
294.66% Cumulative Return
5 yrs
1.69% Cumulative Return
25 yrs
154.29% Cumulative Return
11 yrs
0.83% Cumulative Return
17 yrs
1,059.31% Cumulative Return
17 yrs
0.70% Cumulative Return
11 yrs
50.51% Cumulative Return
5 yrs
1.1897-1.1906
2.1906-6.1924
7.1924-8.1929
9.1929-11.1954
12.1954-1.1966
2.1966-10.1982
11.1982-12.1999
1.2000-12.2010
1.2011-12.2015

Imagine yourself living through these earlier periods. You have 118 years to choose from. Let's consider how your retirement savings would have fared through a couple of these trends.

- If you had retired in 1906 and put your money on Wall Street, looking for interest or dividends for income, and did as well as the DJIA, you would have seen a -4.29% cumulative loss for this 18-year period.
- The period from 1929 to 1954 was the Great Depression. The DJIA gained 1.69% in that 25-year period.
- From 1966 to 1982 you would have captured 0.83% in gains.
- From 2000 to 2010 you would have made 0.70% for this 11–year period.

During these bear market secular trends, you would have been forced to take income by withdrawing from your remaining principal.

The history of the Dow suggests that during your 20–35 years of retirement, you will likely experience firsthand both bear and bull market secular trends (as well the as the multitude of cyclical trends that populate both). Are you prepared?

Just imagine these values applied to air travel. As you board a cross-country flight, you walk past the gate and notice the newly installed *FAA Safe Landing Estimator*. The flashing odds show a 40% chance of landing safely at the end of your flight. Would you still board the airplane?

To be successful in the market, all you must do is make darn sure that your retirement starts at the beginning of a secular bull market trend. Then your primary objective will be not to let a bear market trend interrupt your happiness. This is about as logical as Will Rogers's tongue-in-cheek advice on being a successful stock trader: "Don't gamble. Take all your savings and buy some good stock and hold it till it goes up, then sell it. If it don't go up, don't buy it."

The good health of the market becomes more critical to your success the closer you are to needing a reliable, sustainable retirement income. This is not the time to be playing retirement roulette with your life savings. Lacking a crystal ball or a set of keys to

Mr. Peabody's *Wayback Machine*, we are at the mercy of the *sequence of events*, otherwise known as *timing*. Unless you choose not to be so encumbered.

Can you survive a flawed system? You can indeed, if you want to take control *now*! If you are truly ready for a change to a better arrangement, then you can (1) eliminate the **effects of loss**es of your savings (2) and rid yourself of **excessively high fees and commissions** which are currently eating away at your monthly income as you are reading this book. You can avoid the losses associated with risky investments that have failed before and (3) provide **true diversification** of your assets.

But you will need help from a competent advisor—someone who is licensed to give **advice** and do planning, who can offer you the full spectrum of opportunities that you currently cannot access.

But what about issue (4), Sequence of Events (Timing)? Now there's your trouble. Timing is still a coin toss. *Timing* is the gambling feature at the heart of your retirement savings. Without preventative measures, you are just a river boat gambler. To add the necessary controls, you need to have a game plan—a retirement plan which shows you how to choose the proper financial tools.

To avoid the losses from this flawed system, absolutely must be proactive. You cannot sleep through it.

The above illustration of the DJIA also includes two of the best periods of market growth in history. These were both watershed events that are not likely to be equaled.

- (1) 1924–1929. The five years before the beginning of the Great Depression grew by 294.66%. The period between 1920 and 1929, the Roaring Twenties, was the first time more people lived and worked in cities than on farms. A consumer society was created, driven by nationwide advertising and chain stores. Factories paid higher wages than farms, and more women joined the workforce. Both incomes and personal wealth grew. Well, at least for a while they did.

- (2) 1982–2000. This seventeen-year period increased by 1,059.31%. The period enjoyed great economic prosperity and ended with the bursting of the dot-com bubble.

One of the biggest contributors to the 1982–2000 growth was the adoption of 401(k)s by most American businesses. Starting in the late 1970s, 401(k)s began replacing company pensions. This placed the burden on employees to save their money for retirement, assisted by voluntary employer contributions. In pensions, the risk to the pool of funds and the monthly income was carried by the business. And most of the pension money was held in conservative positions outside of Wall Street. But now, in 401(k)s invested with Wall Street, the employee assumes 100% of the stock market risk to their savings. Suddenly savers became speculators, and all their money began shifting to Wall Street.

> "A total of 84,350 pension plans have vanished since 1985. This figure shocked Pulitzer Prize-winning authors Donald L. Barlett and James W. Steele, who just released their latest book, 'The Betrayal of the American Dream.' Steele

> says there is another number we should pay attention to: $17,686.[10] That's the median value of 401(k) accounts in 2011. For most working people, the amount in their 401(k) account would pay them less than $80 a month for life.
>
> 'What's happening with retirement is almost parallel to what you see happening in other parts of the economy,' says Steele."
> **"Where Did All Our Pensions Go?" *AFL-CIO NOW*, 10/07/2012.**

Check out this incredible statistic:

> "The percentage of workers in the private sector whose only retirement account is a defined benefit pension plan is now 4%, down from 60% in the early 1980s."
> **"Ultimate Guide to Retirement." *CNN Money*, U.S.**[11]

---

[10] The median 401(k) account balance was $18,127 at the end of 2014.
[11] http://money.cnn.com/retirement/guide/pensions_basics.moneymag/index7.htm

A *Towers Watson* study found that from 1998 to 2013, the number of Fortune 500 companies offering traditional defined benefit plans (*pensions*) dropped 86 percent, from 251 to 34.

## Pensions in the Stock Market!?!

Pension funds had always been limited to more conservative investments held out of Wall Street's reach. But times have changed.

> "The funds' managers prudently manage assets in a method meant to ensure that retirees receive promised benefits. For many years, this meant that funds were limited to investing primarily in government securities, investment-grade bonds, and a small amount placed in blue-chip stocks. *Changing market conditions and the need to maintain a high rate of return have resulted in pension plan rules that allow investments in most asset classes.*"
> **Where Do Pension Funds Typically Invest? *Investopedia*, August 31, 2016**

## How Wall Street Wrecked United's Pension

The failure of United Airline's Pension was only a sad story until I met a retired United Airline pilot. He came in with my one of my clients. The photos of aircraft in my office started a conversation which led to his discounted pension benefits. Hearing from a victim took the story from black and white to full color. He did everything right, but others' foolishness and greed cost him the pension he had worked for and deserved—along with the enjoyment and confidence it would have brought.

> "While the money managers and other pension professionals who ran United's pension plan walked away from the wreck unscathed—indeed, they collected about $125 million in fees over the last five years alone, records show—the ones who will have to pick up the bill for the advisers' collective failure will be the airline's 130,000 employees and pensioners, the federal pension guarantor and probably, someday, the taxpayers."
>
> **How Wall Street Wrecked United's Pension. *The New York Times*, July 31, 2005**

Today both 401(k) savings and pensions are more volatile than ever, and controlled by events and conditions completely beyond your control.

*"Change is inevitable.*
*Growth is intentional."*

***Glenda Cloud***

# Chapter 3: What Happens in Argentina Doesn't Stay in Argentina

When I was a single young man fresh out of high school, a cute girl invited me to a party. Obviously, I accepted. The gathering was about 15 miles out of town near a state park in Southwestern Arkansas, and it was to include a bonfire plus food and beverages. When we neared the location, I pulled onto a gravel side road to recover two beers from my trunk. Just then a sheriff's car pulled up and my date panicked. She told me in a high-pitched voice that her dad is a cop too—specifically, an alcohol beverage control officer. "He'll get in trouble and I will too!" This news and my desire to avoid a *minor in possession of alcohol* ticket primed me to leave the area, so I did so.

Sometimes you find yourself with just not quite enough of something. But that was not the case this Friday night: there was an overabundance of both horsepower and adrenaline. During our sojourn back into town, we left the sheriff's car far behind in the dark. But as we slowly drove past the City Limits sign we began to collect other cars—three city police cars, as I recall. Then there was a roadblock followed by a night in jail. (A bad decision, but a good life lesson.)

The moral of this story is, "You may be able to outrun the sheriff's Ford, but you cannot outrun his Motorola!"

## Bad News Equals Big Losses

Wireless communications are still causing problems today. They have progressed light years since the above-described foolish act, turning planet Earth into a village when it comes to getting the *news*. Today we know what's happening everywhere, and it is not very pleasant. What's going on in faraway places affects our minds, our moods and our psyches. That in turn impacts the stock market, your retirement savings and your monthly income.

Why? Because scared people don't buy. They sell. If most those who deal in the market are optimistic, the market does well. If they are pessimistic, it tanks.

Bad news from almost anywhere in the world can directly affect your money. The panic on Wall Street that sabotages your lake house purchase or fantasy world cruise may have had its genesis in a cave in Afghanistan with the hatching of a terrorist plot. Or perhaps it was the seismic shift of tectonic plates beneath the Pacific Ocean that generated the catastrophic tsunami that devastated Japan, killing thousands and destroying homes and businesses (including a nuclear power plant). Or it could have been yet another senseless mass murder of innocent people. Or what separated you from your new motorhome may have been as benign as the latest domestic jobs report.

If Argentina cannot service their debt ... if the people of Cypress wake up to only $300 in their bank accounts ... if there is yet another atrocity in Africa ... if there is a gang war in Mexico ... or if slaves in Asia are processing our seafood ... those events impact the stock market. Bad news both foreign and domestic can directly affect your retirement savings. The cost of subsidizing individuals, businesses, and governments that spend more they can afford is always in the news and can cost you dearly.

And far too often what happens *inside* of Wall Street is the source of the bad news.

## Regarding the Mortgage Crisis / Housing Bubble

> "When the dust settled from the collapse, five Trillion dollars in pension money, real estate value, 401K, savings and bonds had disappeared. Eight million people lost their jobs, six million lost their homes. And that was just in the USA."
>
> ***The Big Short* movie, end credits text**

## A Perfect Storm for PG&E and Bob

Richard and Bob, two retirees from major energy company PG&E, attended one of my programs. We repositioned Richard's 401k money for the safety of principal and market-based gains. The money grew from 2001 through 2010, never taking a loss, accruing profits, and paying out only the required minimum distributions (RMD) after he turned 70½. Richard passed away suddenly, and his IRA money was distributed between two sons and two granddaughters as their inherited IRAs. It continues to grow on a tax-deferred basis, out of the reach of Wall Street. To keep the IRAs tax-deferred, they are required only to take a small RMD based on their life expectancy.

The other retiree, Bob, kept his money in his 401k invested 100% in company stock. Their stock was considered bulletproof. But the company, caught up in the California electric crisis of 2000-2001, was forced to file for Chapter 11 bankruptcy in 2001. On the heels of this bankruptcy came the hit movie *Erin Brockovich*, depicting an environmental contamination law suit that the company settled back in 1996 for $333 million. The combination of these two newsworthy events kept the company in the headlines and made for a perfect storm for PG&E stock, which plummeted. Even though the stock eventually recovered, Bob had to return to work for several years so he could have an income while he waited for the lost value of his company stock to grow back with new gains.

Bad news both foreign and domestic can dramatically impact your monthly income during retirement.

Is all of this is out of your control? Is help available? Yes! Do not despair—there are solutions to be had.

First, you need to realize that change is necessary.

# Chapter 4: Financial Solutions

The following illustration shows the most common types of investments and financial tools. As you consider these investments and their characteristics, your choice should not be based on how they work—but rather, how they work for you. The main criterion for choosing a financial product should be how it will provide what **you** need, how it can help accomplish your personal goals. A proper needs analysis and assessment is required.

The left side shows **investments**, which are at market risk for a higher possible gain. The right side shows **financial tools**, which offer principal protection. These are for the portion of your savings that you cannot afford to lose.

Let's consider their benefits and the limitations.

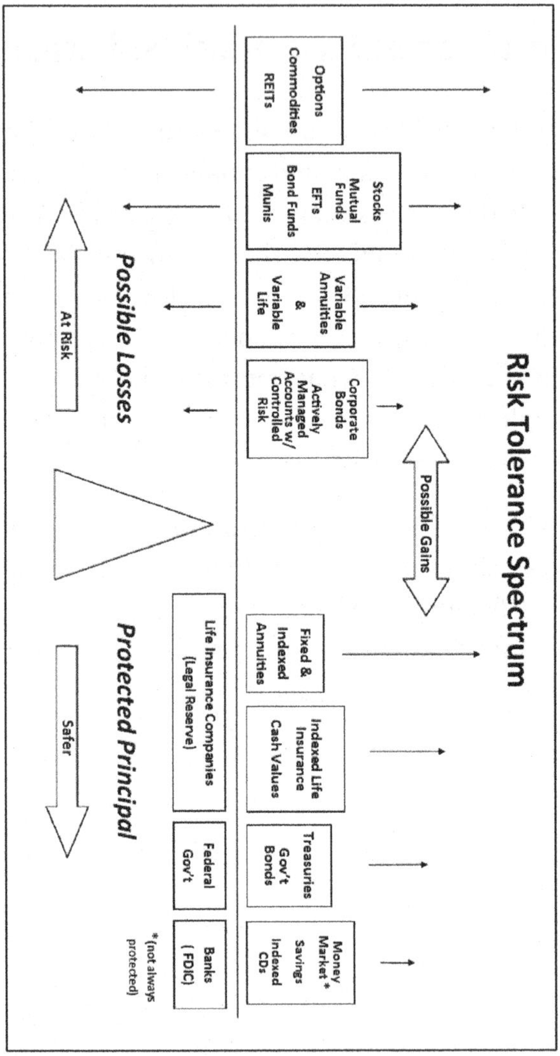
Risk Tolerance Spectrum
Possible Gains
Options
Commodities
REITs
Stocks
Mutual Funds
EFTs
Bond Funds
Munis
Variable Annuities
&
Variable Life
Corporate Bonds
Actively Managed Accounts w/ Controlled Risk
Fixed & Indexed Annuities
Indexed Life Insurance
Cash Values
Treasuries
Gov't Bonds
Money Market *
Savings
Indexed CDs
Possible Losses
At Risk
Protected Principal
Safer
Life Insurance Companies
(Legal Reserve)
Federal Gov't
Banks
( FDIC)
*(not always protected)

## Financial Tools with Principal Protection

### Savings Accounts

As you know, banks are backed by the Federal Deposit Insurance Corporation (FDIC). Credit unions have similar backing by the National Credit Union Share Insurance Fund (NCUSIF). We all need the services of banks and credit unions because we all need liquidity. You need cash for emergencies and opportunities.

Liquidity is typically a small portion of your money. Don't let yourself become so dissatisfied with low interest rates you take too much risk for a couple points of interest. Interest rates will recover with time.

### Government Bonds (Treasuries)

Bonds are debt securities. By purchasing a government bond, you have effectively loaned the government money. Treasury bonds are backed by the good faith of the federal government.

### Indexing: Growth Without All the Drama

Indexing is a method available for use with *CDs, Annuities* and *Life Insurance Cash Values* to capture market-based gains without risking your principal. Through indexing, these principal-protected financial tools can receive gains based on the upward movement of an external market index (like the S&P 500 or Dow Jones Industrial Average) without exposing your savings to stock market risk. Another term for this is approach is "market linked."

Here's how indexing works. If the S&P 500 has a value of 2,000 at the beginning of the year and increases to 2,200 by the end of that year, the gain is 10%. A typical index strategy should include **one** of these limiting factors:

- a **Participation**, expressed as a percentage of how much of the gain you will be credited,
- a **Cap**, the maximum value that you will receive for a set period, or
- a **Spread**, a deduction from the increase.

For example:

- If the indexed strategy makes a 10% gain with an 80% **participation**, you will receive 8% (10% x 80% = 8%). That's your annual gain.

- An annual **cap** of 6% would be the maximum that you could gain if the index made 10%.
- A **spread** strategy of 2% would be subtracted from the 10% gain, leaving you with an 8% gain. (Similar to a spread is an *Asset Fee*—it too would be deducted from the gain, but could carry a charge even if the index strategy declines.)

**Calculating an Index Gain**

Strategy: S&P 500 Monthly Average, with 100% Participation

| | |
|---|---|
| Ending Value: | 1198.657 (October 11, 2004) |
| Beginning Value: | 1124.390 (October 11, 2005) |

Total Annual Gain: 74.267 ÷ 1124.390 = **6.61%**

*Annual Reset* is a feature included in many index strategies. In a downward market trend, this allows for the new year's strategy to begin with the previous year's low ending. Remember, since your principal is protected, your worst outcome is 0% for the year.

## When Zero is Your Hero

On March 10, 2008, we transferred Sandra's savings from mutual funds into an index annuity in order to protect her principal. The S&P 500 was at 1273.37. By the next anniversary of March 10, 2009, it had fallen to 719.60. Sandra received 0% for this period, not particularly good news—until she spoke with her friends and relatives whose losses were considerable. They had all participated in the losses as the S&P 500 gave up 37% of its value. Sandra's next year began at the ending value of 719.60 and grew to 1145.61 by the next anniversary (March 10, 2010), netting her a 25.33% gain. Her strategy was the monthly average of the S&P 500 with a 60% Participation, with annual reset.

Which was more important: her zero for year one (due to the floor under her money) or the nice growth of the second year? The zero was better by far. People who suffered losses had to grow their money back on a reduced basis. (See Understanding the True Impact of Losses in chapter 2.)

Important: Do not confuse the above-described *principal protected* "indexed" financial tools with an **Index Mutual Fund**. Those are securities, and fall under the *non-principal–protected* category.

## Indexed or "Market-Linked" Certificates of Deposit

These CDs are underwritten by major banks, but are not available through local bank branches. The most common types are ***stock-based*** and ***market-linked or -indexed*** for their growth. Those that are stock-based will use a stock (or multiple stocks) as their strategy. Market-linked or -indexed will use an external market index like the S&P 500 or the Dow Jones in their strategy. These include longer time commitments and are not liquid until they mature.

## Annuities

An annuity is a contract offered by a life insurance company for saving and growing money. Money in an annuity grows tax-deferred, requires a time commitment, and can be transferred to another annuity contract tax-free via a 1035 tax-free exchange. If the money is taken out by the owner, left to a beneficiary or moved to another type of financial product, ordinary income taxes are due on the gains.

Of the four basic types of annuities, three offer principal protection: **Immediate**, **Fixed** and **Fixed-Indexed**. The fourth type of annuity is a **Variable**, which is a security and a direct stock market investment, with the associated market risk. With Variables, money is invested into mutual fund subaccounts or separate accounts. Variables are investments with no principal protection.

*Annuities with Principal Protection*

In the three types of annuities providing principal protection, the client's money is held in long-term, high-grade bonds and reserved at around 105%. To meet legal reserve requirements, the life insurance company must have the capacity to match each $100 placed in the annuity by the owner with an equal or greater amount of their money, which averages about $105. The life insurance company cannot withdraw their $105 until they return the $100 to the client. Additionally, in principal protected annuities no sales commissions are paid out of the client's money. The company gains income from bond investments and pays sales commissions from their bond income.

Annuities are backed by the claims-paying ability of the companies that issue them. The annuities which are backed by company guarantees should be included in your state's Guarantee Association Act.

(1) A **Fixed Annuity** is like a CD. It has a simple fixed rate for a fixed period: 3 years, 5 years, 7 years and so on. Some offer a bonus for the first year. These are a favorite of savers who are risk-averse and want to make more than banks are paying, while growing their savings on a tax-deferred basis. Multiple annuities are sometimes laddered to vary their maturity dates. At maturity, the principal and tax-deferred gains can be

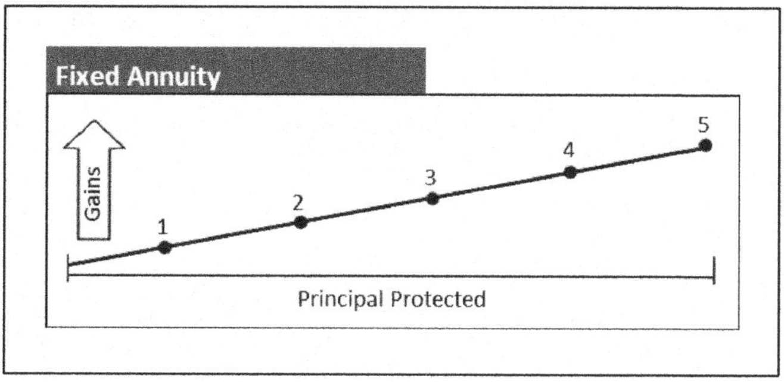

transferred to another annuity without paying taxes via a 1035 tax-free exchange.

(2) An **Immediate Annuity** starts paying right away, like a pension. If issued on a "Life Only" basis it will pay out at the highest rate in a stream of *income for life*, but at the death of the annuitant no money remains. These are relatively rare. It is more common to take a life payout, but to include a declared term of "certain" years so the remaining funds go to one's beneficiaries. The payout rate would be less. In a "Life with 5 Years Certain" contract, if the annuitant died in the second year then the balance of the money would be paid out to his beneficiaries over the remaining years. These contracts are available in 5, 10, 15 or 20 "years certain" periods. They require annuitization, which means the pool of money is exchanged to the life

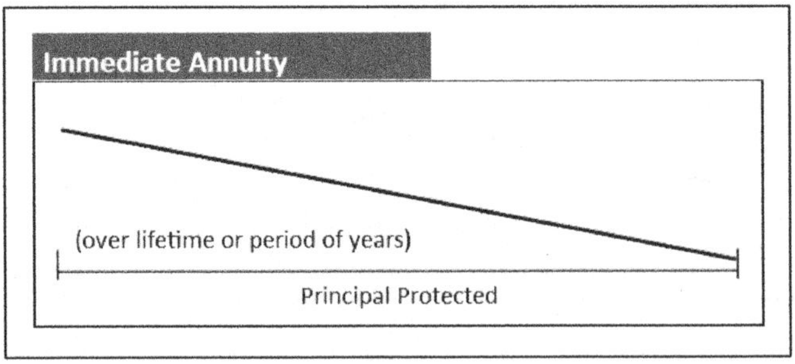

insurance company for a stream of income. In some states, there may be a tax on annuitizations.

(3) An **Indexed Annuity** will include the choice of a fixed-rate option, so these have come to be known

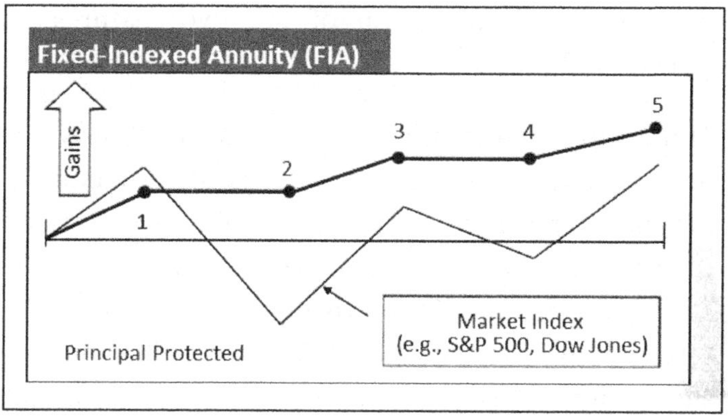


commonly as **Fixed-Indexed Annuities**, **FIAs**, **Equity Indexed** and **Market-Linked.** To simplify things I'll use the term FIA.

The growth of the money in an FIA is linked to the upward movement of an external market index (like the S&P 500 or the Dow Jones) without exposing the retirement savings to a position of direct market risk. FIAs offer a selection of indexed strategies to choose from, and the owner can change or remix index strategies yearly. Common indexes used include the S&P 500, Dow Jones Industrial Average, EuroStoxx50, Russell2000, NASDAQ100, Nikkei 225, and more. When a Lifetime Income Rider is added, the term *Hybrid* is sometimes used to describe the combination of the two features of growth and income.

Third-party information is an excellent way to receive unbiased information about a financial product. The *Real World Index Annuity Returns* report (from Wharton Financial Institutions Center at the University of Pennsylvania) shows real-world returns on fixed-indexed annuities. The figures shown in the report are based on the growth of 172 different indexed-annuity contracts from 19 different life insurance companies during a 12-year period. This period, from 1997 to 2010, included the market loses of 2000 to 2002 (-50%) and 2008 (-37%). The annual returns ranged from 5% to 7% for annualized five-year periods. View the report at https://papers.ssrn.com/sol3/papers.cfm?abstract_id=1482023.

*It's All About Monthly Income!*

Simply put, the goal in retirement planning is to raise a big chicken and then learn to live off the eggs. If you start dining on poultry, you'll soon see the end of your money. Establishing a secure monthly income is vital.

One of the unique features available on annuities and life insurance cash values are *Lifetime Income Riders.* Even if all the money has been depleted, the monthly income payments continue for life. A "rider" is an optional feature to a life insurance policy or an annuity contract that gives an added benefit (typically for an associated fee). The Lifetime Income Rider is a separate value from the "initial premium" paid to the company which is receiving indexed growth. This income rider value will grow at a fixed annual rate, (typically 3% to 8%, or by bonuses added) to develop a larger *basis*—the pool of money used to determine the lifetime monthly income. These gains are commonly called *roll-ups*. This basis may not be accessed except by the income payout, much like the basis of a pension. The growth in the monthly income depends on two separate factors:

1. The longer you wait, the higher the value of the basis becomes. This is the ***roll-up*** or growth period.

2. The older you become, the higher the percentage of monthly payment will become. This is the ***payout*** period.

John's Lifetime Income Benefit Rider began with $250,000 at age 55. He retired at age 66. His **Lifetime Income Benefit** grew as shown:

$250,000
x 6% (*roll-up*) per year
x 11 years
= **$474,574 (A).**

His **Annual Benefit Payout** grew as shown:

| Age 55-59 | Age 60-64 | Age 65-69 | Age 70-74 |
|---|---|---|---|
| 4% | 4.5% | **5% (B)** | 5.5% |

John retired at 66 and began his Lifetime Income:

| | |
|---|---|
| $474,574 | Lifetime Benefit Rider **(A)** |
| 5% | Annual Percentage **(B)** |
| **$23,728** | **Annual Lifetime Income** |

*How a Hybrid Annuity Works*

This is how the average hybrid annuity works. There are many variations on this theme, and this is only an example. Look at the illustration on the next page, and then the explanations for each of the numbers on the illustration:

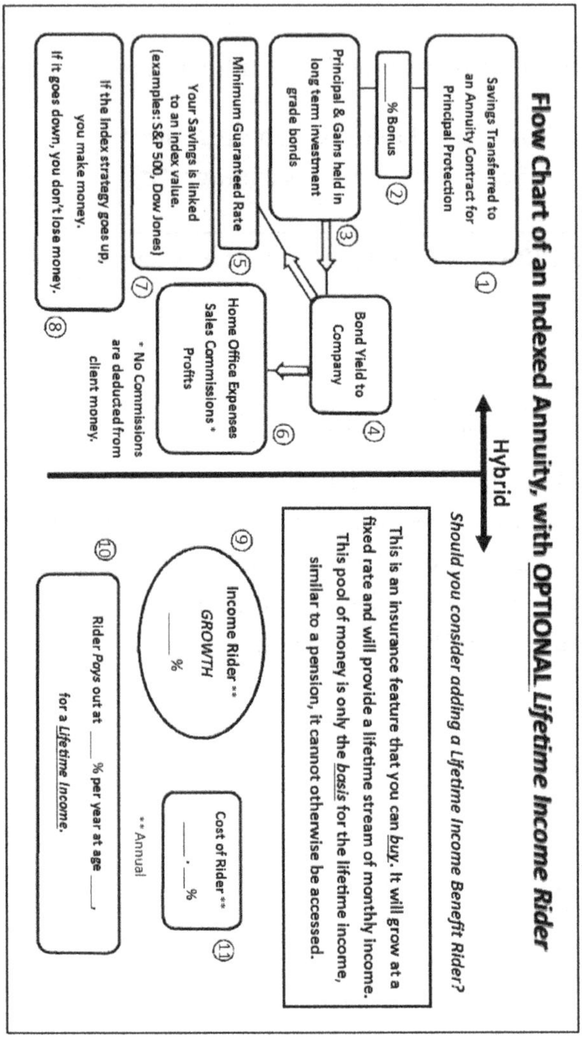
Flow Chart of an Indexed Annuity, with OPTIONAL Lifetime Income Rider
Should you consider adding a Lifetime Income Benefit Rider?
Hybrid
Savings Transferred to an Annuity Contract for Principal Protection
1
____% Bonus
2
Principal & Gains held in long term investment grade bonds
3
Bond Yield to Company
4
Minimum Guaranteed Rate
5
Home Office Expenses
Sales Commissions *
Profits
6
* No Commissions are deducted from client money.
Your Savings is linked to an index value. (examples: S&P 500, Dow Jones)
7
If the Index strategy goes up, you make money.
If it goes down, you don't lose money.
8
This is an insurance feature that you can buy. It will grow at a fixed rate and will provide a lifetime stream of monthly income. This pool of money is only the basis for the lifetime income, similar to a pension, it cannot otherwise be accessed.
9
Income Rider **
GROWTH
____%
10
Rider Pays out at ____% per year at age ____,
for a Lifetime Income.
Cost of Rider **
____ . ____%
11
** Annual

(1) Money transfers into the contract and becomes principal protected. It is now referred to as premium.

(2) An upfront bonus is sometimes offered and there may be a vesting arrangement included. Don't be distracted by a bonus and fail to consider the details of the strategies offered.

(3) The premium is held in high grade bonds and reserved at approximately 105% legal reserve.

(4) The life insurance company takes the bond yield as their income.

(5) They cover the minimum guaranteed rate.

(6) This bond yield pays the company's expenses and their profits. This also pays the agents' sales commissions and is the reason that sales commissions are not deducted from client money.

(7) The premium is linked to an external market index like the S&P 500, Dow Jones, or many others that can be offered. The index value will be recorded along with date of inception of the contract.

(8) The beginning index value will be compared with the value at the anniversary. If the index value goes up, the owner is credited with the gain, per the strategy. If the index value declines, the owner does not lose value because their account value is not in the market—it is in bonds. Should the index value decline, in strategies with an annual reset feature the next year will begin with the low ending value of the previous year. Index strategies can be switched or blended at anniversaries. An owner may typically withdraw 10% per year from the annuity contract. To create a perpetual income a lifetime income rider is added.

(9) The income rider will generally ***roll-up*** at a given percentage or with bonuses added

yearly.

**(10)** The percentage of ***pay-out*** also increases with age. The values of the ***roll-up*** and ***pay-out*** are frozen when the income is begun. The benefit of adding a lifetime income rider is not outliving your money.

**(11)** An annual cost for this feature is typically deducted from the index based gains.

*"I'm Getting 6% a Year Regardless of What the Market Does!"*

No, you're not! Or at least not that you can take out as a lump sum.

I cannot tell you how many times I've heard that first comment above. Some salespeople are leading people astray. The annual additions or *roll-ups* on fixed-indexed and variable annuities are solely to increase the *income basis* for the lifetime payout. This is the value or *basis* on which the monthly income payout will be based, as shown above. This basis is not available as a lump sum. Much like the value that supports pension payments, when the pensioner dies no pool of money goes to beneficiaries (except for survivor's benefits payable to a spouse).

Now, **buyer beware.** There has been tremendous growth in the use of FIA products over the past several years:

- 2013 – $39 billion
- 2014 – $48 billion
- 2015 – $54 billion
- 2016 Q1 & Q2 – $30 billion

But not all products are created equal. Many of these annuities offer very limited growth strategies with little opportunity for index-based gains. They focus more on the value of the Lifetime Income Riders, which generates lifetime income. These riders are indeed valuable planning tools, but indexed gains are also important. Receiving the indexed gains means that you are replenishing at least a portion of what you are drawing out in monthly income. During rate droughts, income strategies have sometimes performed not as well as I would have preferred.

Dan was 68 when he came into my office with a new Fixed Indexed Annuity illustration. The indexing income was capped at 3% after the first year, and could drop down to 2%. So, most of what that company would be paying him was a percentage of his principal—granted, he would indeed continue getting the same monthly income for his lifetime, even if his savings had been exhausted. Take into consideration your beneficiaries when selecting any financial tool or investment.

*Why Do Brokers Hate Annuities?*

You must consider the source of such hatred. Review the growth of fixed-indexed annuities: more than **$171,000,000,000** (billion) in the last three and a half years. That's a lot of money pouring out of Wall Street, coming from clients seeking ways to protect their life savings from stock market losses and generate a lifetime stream of income. The graying of America is in full swing. The baby boomers—an estimated 77 million born between 1946 and 1964—are now retiring. Most do not have pensions, and are seeking ways to support themselves financially without losses. Many players within the financial services industry are competing for these retirement dollars.

Let's put these abstract thoughts into real dollars and common sense. Say you hand over $100,000 to your broker for 20 years. If you make a 3% annual gain, and the broker only charges you 2% annually (including his fee, the cost of the investment and the associated 12b-1 fees), and if you have *no losses* for 20 years, you will end up with $120,577. Oh, and you will have paid your broker $60,034 in fees. Moreover, if this wasn't a pre-tax account (like an IRA) then you would also get a 1099 every year and pay taxes on your annual gains.

But with a $100,000 annuity (that your broker hates), over 20 years at a 3% annual gain you end up with $180,611. You never worried about losses, since your principal and earnings were never at risk. You are $60,034 richer—because that money stayed with you, not your broker.

Remember, the life insurance companies that issue annuities and life insurance hold the money in long-term high-grade bonds. They gain income from these bonds and pay sales commissions from it, so the commissions do not impact the owner's money. The annuity owner gets paid the fixed rate of 3%, or the gains from the index strategy. Also, annuities grow your money on a tax-deferred basis. You would have received not one 1099 nor paid taxes for that 20-year period (unless you spent some of the money). Your money, including the gains, can be moved from one annuity to another via a 1035 tax-free exchange.

The broker's hatred of annuities is monetarily based. He is concerned about the loss of his personal income, not about the above benefits that favor you.

Here are two questions for the broker that hates annuities.

1. Can you protect my principal from market losses, while providing me with market-based gains linked to a major market index, like the S&P 500 and the Dow Jones, and when I need it, generate a stream of monthly income for me which I cannot outlive?

2. Is what you did for me worth $60,034?

*Indexed Life Insurance and Cash Value*

The cash values in this special class of principal protected life insurance policies can be overfunded, grow by indexed-based gains, pay out a *lifetime* of tax-free income, leverage the death benefit value to pay for Long Term Care and pay a tax-free legacy to your heirs outside of probate. This is a favorite tool used by serious advisors.

For Helen, who was 70 at the time, we repositioned $159,053 from mutual funds into an indexed life insurance policy. This leveraged a death benefit of $347,759. No future premiums are required and she has access to her money. The real benefits are (1) avoiding losses to her savings and getting control of taxes, (2) generating an indexed based tax-free income and (3) establishing a tax-free benefit which can be passed on to her heirs outside of probate.

As a bonus, the death benefit value is also available for Long Term Care expenses, starting at $7,576 per month, but only if she needs it. Should this never become necessary, she hasn't paid for something that she'll never use.

One of these three realities will take place, sooner or later....

1. She may live happily ever after spending her tax-free indexed based gains, while being protected from the whims of Wall Street.

2. She may use some of the funds for Long Term Care.

3. She may leave the tax-free death benefit to her children and grandchildren outside of probate.

... or perhaps a combination of the three.

IRA savings can also be used to fund an indexed life insurance policy. The payments would be spread out over a period of years to control the amount of taxes levied. For those that want to avoid Required Minimum Distribution (RMDs) starting at age 70 ½, this will get your savings to a tax-free position for you or for your beneficiaries. These forced RMD payments only go up with age.

But what if you are uninsurable or have health issues which would make the insurance costs prohibitive? You can use another person as the insured and still own the policy and control the features. There are three parties to a life insurance policy, beyond the company. There is the *insured* person, the *owner* of the policy and the *beneficiary*. You can own a life insurance policy on another person if you have an insurable interest in them, including a spouse, a child, a parent, an employee or a business partner. Only a few life insurance policies will effectively deliver all the benefits that are described here.

### *Banks Love Owning Life Insurance*

It's called Bank-Owned Life Insurance (BOLI). The more BOLI a bank has in its Tier One Core Capital, the higher the banks rating becomes. As stated above, the attraction here is that the life insurance company holds the money in long-term high-grade bonds, with an average legal reserve of $105 for every $100 of client money. So, what qualifies as Tier One Core Capital? ***Cash***, ***Gold***, ***Treasuries*** and ***Life Insurance***. Bank-owned life insurance holdings reached $146 billion in 2014.

### *A Few Words about Life Insurance Companies*

Regarding financial clout:

"There are over two thousand different life insurance companies in the United States. Collectively, these companies own, control, or manage more assets than *all the banks in the world combined.* The insurance industry of North America owns, controls, or manages more assets than *all the oil companies in the world combined.* During the Great Depression, it was not the government that bailed out the banking industry; it was U.S. insurance companies. If there were ever a financial collapse in this nation, the insurance industry would be next to last—second only to the government—to fold. And this is only true because the government has taxing power and, of course, the ability to print money. If the insurance industry were ever to collapse, we would look back at the Great Depression as a walk in the park in comparison."

***Getting Started in Annuities* by Gordon K. Williamson**

## Investments Without Principal Protection

### Stock

You are an owner! One of the thrills of owning stock is you get to watch the trading results and know that, perhaps even in a small way, you have ownership in that famous brand and its trading symbol. You may get to participate in equity growth and dividends. You are also at the bottom of the food chain when it comes to failures. Individual stock investments are high up on the volatility list. But there are new, less-volatile methods for investing a portion of your retirement savings in stock.

### Mutual Funds

Instead of investing all your money in just one stock, the purpose of a mutual fund is to provide the spread of risk or diversification among a group of stocks. These are the most common investments used today, and in the last two market crashes, their *diversification* has failed to protect investor money. It is well known throughout the financial services industry that these funds have performed poorly. The majority underperform their benchmarks, which is usually the S&P 500. The S&P 500 outperforms 80% to 90% of mutual funds every year. See also Chapter 2, under "The Failure of Wall Street's Diversification."

> "Over the last 15 years, fewer than 4% of all mutual funds outperformed the S&P 500."
> ***What Wall Street Doesn't Want You To Know***
> **by Larry E. Swedroe**

> "86% of investment managers stunk in 2014. People pay investment managers a lot of money to do one thing: Beat the market. The skills and expertise of fund managers are supposed to give them the ability to select better stocks and bonds than an index like the Dow Jones or S&P 500. The problem is that hasn't been happening lately. A staggering 86% of active large-cap fund managers failed to beat their benchmarks in the last year, according to an S&P Dow Jones Indices scorecard released on Thursday. And no, that wasn't a one-off blip either. Nearly 89% of those fund managers underperformed their benchmarks over the past five years, and 82% did the same over the last decade."
> **CNN Money 3-12-2015**

> "How many mutual funds beat the S&P 500 on a percentage basis after operational fees? Based on the Standard & Poor's Index Versus Active (SPIVA) scorecard as of June 30, 2015, 65.34% of large-cap managers underperformed the S&P 500 for the 1-year period. Over the last 5-year period, 80.8% underperformed the S&P 500. Over the last 10-year period, 79.59% of active managers underperformed."
> ***Investopedia*, March 2016**

Many retirees have concluded that if the S&P 500 Composite Index and other indexes generally outperform the clear majority of mutual funds, why not switch to index strategies? They use CDs, annuities, and life insurance cash values as their financial tools. If you can get 50% to 80% of the upside of the S&P 500, Dow Jones, and many other indexes, with neither market losses nor fees, would that not be preferable?

## Indexed Mutual Fund

These funds are populated with the stocks of a sector index like the S&P 500 Composite Index. Since the indexes generally outperform most mutual funds, indexed mutual funds have become popular among brokers as a substitute. But these too are at market risk because they will rise and fall with the market changes.

## Corporate Bonds

These bonds are debt securities too. Long term high-grade bonds (Investment Grade Bonds) are a foundation to investing. These bonds sustained the life insurance companies through the Great Depression, for the direct benefit of their clients. But to benefit from these bonds the way life insurance companies and other institutions do, you need the life expectancy of a Galapagos sea turtle. Long term means just that. Corporate and government bonds have a finite maturity date—a date when the investor gets a return of their principal if the issuer does not default.

## Bond Funds

Not all bonds are created equal. A bond fund is a mutual fund of bonds. Should you purchase bonds in a bond fund, the originator is not responsible for the trading costs, errors, poor business practices and expenses of the fund manager or his team. Bond funds can be very sensitive to interest rate increases.

With falling interest rates, they do well; but with rising interest rates and a Bond Bubble growing since 2011, many are wary or exiting.

> "'But with higher rates on the horizon and the Federal Reserve slowly reducing the pace of its quantitative easing measures, investors are about to get schooled in just how different these securities can be. For financial advisors who have experienced only a bond market rally in their careers, this promises to be an eye-opener. There is a huge difference between bond funds and individual bonds,' said Scott Colyer, CEO and chief investment officer of Advisors Asset Management. 'Some suggest that they're not even the same asset class because bond funds react so differently to market forces. Now more than ever, with interest rates heading up, investors need to understand the difference,' he said."
> **CNBC, Shelly Schwartz, April 10, 2014**

## Municipal Bonds

These are another form of debt security issued by a municipality: government, state, county, city or on behalf of a local authority. "Muni's" offer tax-free growth. Should you purchase a municipal bond in your state, you should get it free of both federal and state income taxes. This works well for investors in higher income tax brackets. A 4% untaxed gain from a muni nets them more than a 6% taxed gain, which nets them 3% or less.

Although not individually taxed, municipal bond gains will increase your threshold income, raising taxes on other income—including the tax on your Social Security.

Overspending and acquiring too much credit debt has become popular everywhere, including with municipalities. If they cannot budget their money correctly, their bankruptcy can become your problem. The main cause for concern here is the insolvency of so many municipalities. What if your choices go bankrupt as so many have?

### Variable Annuity

This type of annuity is a direct stock market investment, so the values will rise and fall with market activity. The money invested here is in the sub-accounts of mutual funds, sometimes called separate accounts. There are about six variable annuities sold for every annuity providing principal protection. These are a favorite product of Wall Street since they provide high reoccurring revenue in annual fees and trail commissions—all of which are paid from the investor's money.

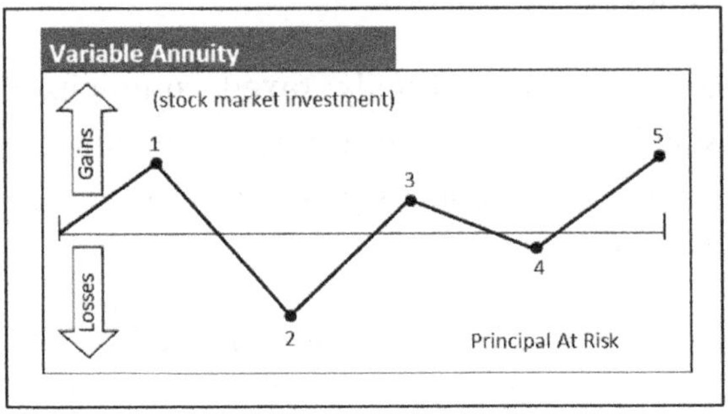


Since variable annuities are volatile, if you purchase one you should also purchase the riders for both death and income. These riders are insurance features which, for an additional cost, deliver certain benefits.

- Death Rider. In the case of the death of the annuitant, any lost value is returned. For instance, if the value had decreased from $100,000 to $75,000 then the rider would pay the beneficiary the original amount of $100,000.

- Income Rider. The income rider protects the original value in a similar way. Should the original value take a market loss from $100,000 down to $75,000, the owner would be able to use the income feature based on the original $100,000. If there were an increasing factor or roll-up on the income value, it too could increase the original value. But should the owner need to withdraw funds from the account value, this would further reduce both its value and the future monthly income payments.

The Real World Indexed Annuity Returns report mentioned above (under fixed-indexed annuities) noted that 1997–2010, variable annuity annual costs averaged 4%. Over the past few years, I have found that total annual expenses on the variable annuities I have reviewed range from 3.25% to 5.25%.

Here are a couple of cases from recent history for your consideration. Remember, the final determination as to whether an investment is good or bad for you is if it satisfies your needs and accomplishes your goals.

*A Little Something for the Kids?*

Sid and Clara have $500,000 in variable annuities. They say the purpose of this money is "to take an income from it for 8 to 10 years and then leave it to our children." They were told that their fees were less than 2%. Here are their actual annual *costs*. You should **always ask for the total costs**.

| | |
|---|---|
| Mortality and Expense "Fee" | 1.45% |
| Death Benefit Rider expense | 0.90% |
| Income Benefit Rider expense (may increase to a max of 2.10%) | 1.05% |
| Investment Accounts fees | 0.95% |
| Total (per year, every year) | **4.35%** |

When I showed them their total annual costs, they said, "We are not paying nearly that much. We would have noticed an annual cost of over $21,000 per year coming out of our money." I pointed out that they had made a whopping 3% over the past year, while the market had been soaring. These costs were being drained from their gains *before* the company prepared their anniversary statement. The actual gain from their variable annuities was probably close to 10% *before costs*. These costs can eat up a lot of your savings. The Dow Jones averaged 10.10% from 2011 to 2015. The inception of their variable annuities was May of 2012. The broker was making more money on this investment than they were, which is common.

Does this investment meet their goal of taking an income and then leaving the balance as a legacy for their children?

Two problems persist.

1. Should the market drop and the investment account gains no longer support the annual costs, they will continue to be paid out of the principal. Thus the need for buying death and income riders, should you consider buying a variable annuity.

2. Many owners never learn about this detail, but their beneficiaries often do: Once they start to take income from the income rider at 4.5% per year, fees and expenses continue.

So, 4.5% in income payout plus 4.35% in costs equals a total annual net deduction of 8.85%. This means that the *account value* will last about eleven years. Granted, the lifetime income payout of 4.5% will be paid out for the lifetimes of the owner and spouse, even if the account value is depleted. But nothing is left for the beneficiaries, their children.

This would have met their needs and goals if all they wanted was the lifetime income. But it does not meet their desire for wealth transfer to their children, nor provide access to their principal for single withdrawals.

Many variable annuities must be annuitized to generate the stream of income. Annuitization occurs when the contract is returned to the company in exchange for a stream of income. No more gains available, just a stream of income until the death of the annuitant.

### *Life Insurance Would Have been a Lot Cheaper and Tax-Free*

Bill and Jane are ranchers. Bill is several years older than his wife. He invested $209,000 in a variable annuity, which had decreased in value to $140,000 by the time they came in to see if I could replace it for them. We contacted the company, and I was told that the 6% surrender charge would be assessed on the original investment value of $209,000 and not just the remaining balance of $140,000. This put it out of reach for recovery. There was a death benefit rider on Bill, but no income rider.

Jane did not understand the gravity of their circumstances, so Bill carefully explained to her that they would not be able to use their retirement savings for travel, which had been their intention. When he died, she would get at least the original $209,000 through the death benefit rider. But if they withdrew any money it would further reduce the current balance of $140,000.

This variable annuity might have met their goals if it had included the income rider, or if they had not put all their retirement savings into it. They had no children to leave their savings to, so the income feature—even though it would have depleted their account value—would have been preferable to just waiting for the death claim payment on Bill.

A death benefit paid from life insurance is tax free. But a death benefit paid from the gain of an annuity is taxed as ordinary income. This can be softened by a multi-year payout.

*Return on Deposit*

Bob and Tina became clients in 2004. I repositioned their money to reduce its volatility and to build a basis for a lifetime income whenever they should need it. The one account that we left "as is" was a variable annuity that Bob had purchased six years before for $87,000. The value had dropped during the 2000-2002 market crash to a little less than $50,000. When Bob passed away, the 11-year-old variable annuity paid Tina a check for exactly $87,000. Surely a waste of their time and a source of irritation. But on the bright side of things, the money that they did invest in this variable annuity was only a minor portion of their portfolio. Tina is enjoying her retirement thanks to the lifetime income we created for her.

## Actively-Managed Money with Controlled Risk

With this type of investment, you have a hands-on team that actively watches and moves your money for the benefit of the client. Their goal is to get the best of the upside in good times and take you to safety during bad times. There are many variations on this theme. Here's an example for your information.

In this *Model* there are 25 major stocks, which were chosen for their characteristics and how they fit into three stock sectors: *defensive*, *sensitive* and *cyclical.* The manager and his team reposition the money into the sectors that will be the most beneficial for market conditions.

How would you choose an Actively-Managed Money Model? As you should choose anything else: you look at its history. Turn to a third-party independent reporting service like Morningstar® to get accurate, unbiased information. The history of gains and losses is important, but as you already know, "past performance is not a guarantee of future results." What we can rely on for past performance information are two important risk metrics, *Alpha* and *Beta*. These two metrics can tell us how this plan has performed over time relative to a market benchmark. In this case, the benchmark is the S&P 500 Total Return, which includes dividends.

The **Alpha** measures the risk-adjusted performance in relationship to the benchmark. This tells us how well it performed compared to the benchmark and how quickly it has recovered from losses. The S&P 500's Alpha is the standard at 1.0%. We want an Alpha value of *more* than 1.0%.

The **Beta** measures the volatility of this model in relationship to the benchmark. The S&P 500's Beta is 1.0%. We desire a model that is less volatile than the S&P 500, so we want the Beta value to be *less* than 1.0%;

The ten-year averaged risk metrics for this Model are Alpha 4.32 and Beta 0.77. In other words, **this Model has outperformed the S&P 500 TR by 30% for ten years**.

It also comes with an optional *controlled-risk feature*, a 15% stop-loss (just in case Argentina can't service its debt again).

Still, this is an "at risk" investment and should be of limited use with your retirement savings.

The success of an investment model like this is attributed to the skill and experience of the manager and his team. With a team, somebody is always awake and in control, whereas an individual can sometimes get sleepy.

*Red Toenail Polish, Punishment for the Sleepy*

We had just finished an hour-long game of three-way racquetball and walked into the locker room to shower and get dressed. Danny and Bobby were standing as we continued our conversation and I sat down on a bench and took off my shoes. When the socks came off, they stopped talking and stared at my feet. When I looked down to see what had caught their attention I could clearly see that all ten of my toenails were covered in glossy red polish. I stared at my red toes for a long time and finally looking up I said, "I got nothing for you." I was clueless on how my toenails came to be painted with red polish. All I could think to add was, "If I had done this, I would have done a better job." There was as much red polish on my toes as there was on my toenails.

I mentally backtracked through my day: I got up at 6 a.m., jogged 2 miles, ate breakfast, showered and dressed for the office, worked all day, and met the guys at the racquet club. I had changed socks three times and had not noticed the new custom coloring.

So, when I arrived at home, I had a few questions in tow. "Would anybody know just how my toenails got...?" Laughter interrupts me, a chorus of laughter. The guilty parties gave themselves up by their uncontrolled, tearful laughter. The crime was revealed, and I did recall their warning. As we settled in to watch a movie the night before, it was mentioned that if Dad fell asleep *again* during the family movie, there would be repercussions.

And of course, I fell asleep.... *again*.

During my deep sleep, Debbie (wife), Jessica (daughter) and Matthew (son) painted all ten toenails candy-apple red. I was told that as they tried to control their laughter and fought over who got to paint the next toenail, the quality of the work suffered, resulting in an overflow of red.

The answer to your obvious question here is *no*, I'm not the manager of an actively managed model, so don't worry. But I am a fee-based planner and a licensed *advisor,* and I know how to choose quality investments and financial tools for my clients.

## Full Disclosure and Transparency

Any investment (whether an actively managed money model, mutual fund, bond fund, variable annuity or other "at risk" investment program) worth your time and consideration will have their performance audited by a third-party independent reporting service like Morningstar. This will provide you with accurate, unbiased information from which you can make an informed choice. Going forward, this is the least value that you should accept: all the available, current information with full disclosure and transparency.

If you are dealing with someone licensed to give advice and offer planning, they should be able to explain to you in an understandable manner just how the financial products they are recommending will work for your benefit. Don't let unusual language confuse you. If you don't get it at first, ask for a better explanation until you understand. I'm often reminded of Strother Martin's famous line from the Paul Newman movie *Cool Hand Luke*: "What we've got here is failure to communicate." If someone cannot explain these things to your satisfaction, walk away. There are a lot of junk investments out there. Information is vital and words are important.

**Well, It Matters to the Dog!**

A brown dog showed up at my parents' home one day. Ragged and weary, his bulging ribs showed his hunger. He was an obvious victim of neglect, if not abuse. He was given bowls of food and water. He got a house all his own in the back yard, and even a cushion on the porch. His pleasant nature and facility around the cattle secured him a new home. Mom knew that along with ownership came responsibility, so she called the vet.

"We have a new dog and we need to make an appointment for the shots. Since we don't need a lot of puppies running around here, we need to have the dog fixed too."

The vet's assistant said, "The doctor can see your dog on Thursday at 10:30. So I can prepare the surgery room with the correct instruments, tell me, does your dog need to be *spayed* or *neutered*?"

Without missing a beat Mom replied, "Oh, honey, I don't care—whichever is the cheapest." Words matter.

***Your Retirement Workbook*** (described in Chapter 6) includes the questions needed to develop your assessment and needs analysis. When completed, it will aid a licensed advisor in determining the best blend of investment vehicles and financial tools to satisfy your needs and accomplish your goals.

But here's where a common problem exists. Some people have not developed the skills to accept improvement.

# Chapter 5: Failure to Launch

## Why Is It So Hard to Make a Change?

One of the most difficult things for some people to do is *change*. Change is hard even where there are obvious benefits, such as shifting away from volatility toward security or swapping pain for comfort. But I have seen so many remain in the worst investments and lose their money because they could not bring themselves to the point of deciding to *change*.

It's like watching someone throw back their catch of a 30-inch salmon and go hungry just because all they own is a 12-inch skillet. I suggest that most of the difficulty in deciding to change is lack of information and fear of the unknown. With a little effort on your part and some direction, you can overcome this challenge.

Not knowing what to do while facing serious financial risk can be daunting. Jim from Chapter 1 would freeze up upon suffering losses. He did not know what else to do. He had already run the full gamut of brokers in the area and found no benefit. Though he was unaware of it at the time, he accomplished nothing. He was moving his money in and out of the same products, only with different-colored labels. It's not uncommon to see where people have panicked out of the lack of a better option. Not finding a solution to their problem, they freeze-up. People who bring in two or three of their monthly brokerage statements and ask me to open the statements for them have frozen in the same manner.

## Motivation to Change

Consider this your opportunity for a positive change. This is a way to protect your retirement savings and the income you will need. More than anything, acquiring knowledge will give you the power to make sound choices. The more you know, the better you can decide. Information can give you the insight to choose your new direction.

Understand the gravity of the situation. This is more than you making a choice between gas stations—this is your financial future. If your retirement savings is at too much risk, there is another path.

You can either fix this now or suffer the consequences later.

Usually the husband takes the lead in investing for a couple. A question that I always like to ask is, "In *your* absence, who will your wife turn to for advice and direction?" Someone not licensed to give advice? A plan can include an *autopilot*-type feature to satisfy this concern.

## Put a Face on Your Money

While I was visiting with a couple, the wife made light of a $16,000 mutual fund loss during the last quarter. She had bought into Wall Street's "we must live with losses" mentality. When I replied, "No, you didn't lose $16,000," she looked puzzled. I explained, "What was taken away from you was a 15 day Australia-New Zealand cruise in a suite with a balcony, first class round-trip airfare included." You should have seen her face. It was the first time she had measured their monetary losses by more than the changes in printed values.

You need to see the value of a well-thought-out retirement game plan and the benefits, protection and income it can offer.

## How to Check Out a New Advisor

It is easy to do your due diligence in gathering information on someone you anticipate entrusting with your money and future income. If you are considering investing your retirement savings with someone at least *check them out*. I do work for a lot of people that I have never met in person. I have clients from Alaska to Virginia; it was easy for all of them to *check me out*.

Here are three reporting services that you can contact.

- **The Better Business Bureau.** The local BBB is the most common way to check out customer relations. What's their rating? Are there any complaints which have not been satisfied?

- **National Ethics Association.** The NEA systematically does annual background checks for both civil and criminal activity for all members. They also check for complaints on both security and insurance licenses.

- **Broker Check.** FINRA (Financial Industry Regulatory Authority) hosts a website where you can view the history of people with securities licenses.

All three of these are accessible from the front page of my website. If the individual you are considering doesn't subscribe to these, why does he not?

## Why You Need to Check Them Out

About eight years ago, a news article appeared on the front page of the local paper about a Real Estate Investment Trust (REIT) that had taken tens of millions of dollars from local investors in a Ponzi Scheme. At the bottom of the article, one of the victims said, "I guess we should have checked them out." If they had, they would have found a history of securities fraud.

Last year Bill*, a new client who had been getting resistance from his broker in releasing his funds for transfer, shared a story with me. Bill said that when his broker could not offer what I had recommended, in frustration the broker said, "Well, let's just check this guy out" (meaning me). There were no problems found. But when Bill got home, he went on the same website to check out his current broker—and found he had a long history of complaints.

## Questions for Your Prospective Advisor

### Are You Licensed To Give or Sell *Financial Advice*?

Most of Wall Street's investments are purchased from someone who is not licensed to provide advice or do financial or retirement planning. Does this make sense to you? Purchasing financial products without knowing how they will work for you in your overall game plan is like buying a car from someone who has never learned to drive, or taking pilot training from someone without a pilot's license. Obtaining maximum performance from your retirement savings requires the coordination of a mix of investments and financial tools, providing you with an enjoyable retirement. Ensuring a successful outcome requires a game plan, and a game plan requires advice and planning.

### What Is Your Work History and Experience?

There's no substitute for experience. Too many of those selling investments today have not lived through enough secular market trends to understand the value of a well-thought-out game plan for your retirement.

### Are You Independent? Or Are You Employed by (or Contracted to) One Insurance Company or Broker-Dealer?

A *captive employee* can only sell from the inventory of their employer. This is very limiting. Single source employees are not free and able to access investments and financial tools that retirees need. This is an area where high-cost, low-performance *proprietary funds* are often promoted.

## What Types of Financial Products Do You Use?

Where do you place most of your client's retirement savings? Do you offer principal protected products?

## What Services Do You Offer?

Do you provide tax-reduction, income and estate distribution planning? Can you get my IRA to my children and grandchildren on a tax-favored basis? Can you help me choose the best way to take Social Security?

## How Do You Get Paid?

What is the total *cost* deducted from my savings for your services? Are you fee- or commission-based? If I'm losing money, do you still get paid?

## Have You Ever Received Public Discipline?

This is an area that you need to explore before you sign on. If you see something out of the ordinary, ask about it.

## Are You Experiencing Excessive Broker Loyalty?

The choice here is not between people, but rather between business models. Which will deliver what you need? We all make friends and develop relationships. Nobody appreciates this more than I do. As mentioned earlier, I left the broker-dealer world so I could provide a more holistic approach to retirement planning for my clients. I wanted to offer the more conservative securities-based investments and alternative financial tools that my clients needed as they got older—products which included principal protection, along with market-based gains and lifetime income strategies. These are just not available through Wall Street.

Your broker is aware of these products. He has lost accounts to licensed advisors like myself—probably a lot of accounts. But he has decided to ignore the value of these products and the benefits of planning for his older clients. He continues to sell the Wall Street status quo. Why? Could it be for the reoccurring commissions that he has accumulated over the years? Perhaps he doesn't quite understand how important it is that retirees protect their retirement savings from market downturns. Like the downturn in 2008, where over $5 trillion was lost—$5,000,000,000,000! This suggests what Upton Sinclair quipped: "It is difficult for a man to understand something when his paycheck depends on him not understanding it."

Are you impressed by the large buildings with well-advertised names, buildings that your dollars are helping pay for? Have you noticed how often their occupants—national investment banks and broker-dealers—show up on the news because of poor business practices and investment management misdeeds? Still, some retirees stay with the same status quo investments (which failed in the last two market crashes) for the perceived value of a gain, while ignoring the hazards and pitfalls of the losses.

## Bubba and the Outhouse

It was a bitterly cold, frosty morning in the hills of Eastern Oklahoma, back during the Great Depression. Mr. Johnson walked out into his field to check on his livestock. A tapping noise caught his attention, and he turned to look. At a distance, he could see the neighbor's boy Bubba in his shirtsleeves, poking at something in the top of the family's outhouse. Knowing Bubba, Mr. Johnson thought it best to go and see if he could help—or at least avoid calamity. As he walked closer, he could see that Bubba was *fishing* in the outhouse with a cane pole. Chuckling to himself, he hollered, "Bubba, son, there are no fish in an outhouse." Being a respectful young man, Bubba replied, "Yes sir, Mr. Johnson, I know there are no fish in the outhouse. Sir, on accident, I dropped my best winter coat down the hole, and I'm just trying to fish it back out." That shocked the old man. What had seemed at first to be humorous had taken a very serious turn. He put his hand on Bubba's shoulder and said, "Son, you forget about that coat. Your folks will get you another one. In the bottom of this outhouse is filth, disease and contamination—that's the foulest place on earth." Bubba replied to his concerns, "Yes sir, Mr. Johnson. I know it's just awful down in there. I don't think I could ever wear my coat again, even if it were all cleaned-up. Just the thought of it being down there would keep me from putting it back on." Somewhat surprised, Mr. Johnson asked, "Well, boy, if you feel that way, then why are you trying to fish it out?" Bubba looked up at him with a big grin and replied,

"Oh sir, did I not mention? There is a fresh buttered biscuit in the right-hand pocket!"

Bubba was focused on a basic *want*. The thing he was truly fishing for was one of his mother's buttermilk biscuits, still warm, with a big slice of fresh churned butter inside. He ignored the circumstances that were hazardous to his health.[12]

Many retirees are striving after a perceived value of a possible gain while ignoring the reality of a dismal financial failure.

Are you **prepared for improvements**?

---

[12] This is my embellishment of a story I heard as a kid visiting my grandfather's farm in Oklahoma. Outhouse humor was abundant. Mel Tillis also told a version of it.

# Chapter 6: The Plan, Your Source of Confidence

*"A goal without a plan*
*is just a wish."*

***Antoine de Saint-Exupery***
*(1900 - 1944)*

Times have changed.

I drove to Shreveport, Louisiana with a friend to race my car. We pulled into a gravel parking lot at an outdoor diner for lunch before the event. The carhop hung a metal tray on my door and served up two Cajun-style fried oyster baskets and a *big cold pitcher of beer*. Imagine that today—a business delivering a pitcher of beer to your car. Well, it was back in my high school days, in Louisiana, where the legal drinking age was 18 and we were not.

But times have indeed changed, and the passing of time should change our way of assessing risk. As we get older, most of us become more conservative in our thinking and our actions. We tend to take fewer chances. We have all spent time, money and effort to make sure that all our stuff is safe. We make sure the roof doesn't leak and that the locks and alarms all work. We even buy insurance on the more important things: our homes, our cars and even our lives. We insure everything against *loss*. Well...

...everything except your retirement savings.

Most of the people I meet are still holding their savings in places of high volatility. Most are still in the same investments as their children and grandchildren. They know nothing of the alternatives and new strategies discussed in Chapter 4, nor how these more conservative investments can work for them. Still, we all desire security in this area of our lives. After all, nobody wants to lose their retirement savings. But where can you find security? That is the question.

Financial security typically means one of two things.

- If you're still working, it means having a secure job with a steady paycheck.

- If you're retired, security means having a dependable, reliable, sustainable income stream.

Today the people who are employed to print money seem to have the job security of a central African cartographer. Their only concerns are, "What happens if we run out of ink or paper?"

But the rest of us are on our own. We do have one major choice to consider: We can…

- Sit quietly and wait to see how Wall Street's next shenanigans might affect our savings, how tax increases and the deficit may impact our pre-tax dollars, and how the lack of fiscal responsibility by cities, counties and states (and even Greece and Argentina) can reduce our retirement accounts, *or*

- Develop a plan.

## Why You Need a Game Plan

You would never consider taking a long journey to an unfamiliar land by yourself without a fistful of maps and a GPS. You want reservations too, whether a suite at the Ritz-Carlton or a pad to pitch your tent. In travel, you want to know destinations, routes and dangers. But here you are jumping off into 20 to 35 years of retirement without a proper plan. Forget about not having all the answers—you don't even know all the questions! Security comes from right expectations, knowledge of your options and a good Plan B in your pocket.

You need a *game plan*—a comprehensive retirement plan.

This game plan is not an event. It is a ***process***, one that continues to work for you for life. It is regularly tweaked, polished and updated; it will steer you toward opportunities while helping you avoid irreversible mistakes. When new directions demand to be considered, you will return to your plan to re-magnetize the needle of your financial compass.

Why don't you have a plan? Why are plans so scarce?

You are likely dealing with a Registered Representative whom you refer to as a broker or advisor. A Registered Representative is only licensed to *sell* the investment products in the inventory of his or her broker-dealer employer. They are not licensed or qualified to give or charge for *advice* on financial or retirement matters. Nor can they go outside their employment arrangement to offer clients the full selection of alternatives from the universe of conservative opportunities, such as financial tools providing both principal protection and market-based gains.

You may have received a *Monte Carlo Simulation*, named after the famed gambling mecca. The point of this stack of scenarios is to indicate the likelihood of success (expressed as a percentage) of a long-range financial forecast. How likely is it that today's *at-risk* investment selection will prove successful throughout the next 20–35 years? The weather girl gets tomorrow's forecast wrong on a regular basis, and she knows which way the wind is blowing.

If there was value in this approach, why did most investors lose money in the market crashes of 2000–2002 and again in 2008? What will happen the next time Wall Street goes south? At the end of this approach lies no tactical plan, no hedge, no exit strategy, no safety net, no stop-loss, no tax considerations and surely a stark absence of planning.

Here is the most common substitute for a retirement plan: "Well now, let's just split your hard-earned life savings between high-cost, low-performing mutual funds and risky bond funds, toss them way up into the air and wait to see which direction the economic winds will blow!" The single biggest financial hit you can take is to lose a significant portion of your savings near or during your retirement. By following the above "plan" (or lack thereof), you'll be sure to participate in the next big market downturn.

*"If you don't know where you are going you will probably end up someplace else."*

***Laurence J. Peter***
*(creator of the Peter Principle)*

## Building Your Retirement Game Plan

Before choosing the proper mix of investments and financial tools from Chapter 4, you need to submit to a subjective evaluation, including a needs analysis and assessment. (See ***Your Retirement Workbook***, described below.) Planning starts with an assessment—yes, filling out some forms and answering questions. What are your concerns, goals, needs, timeline and risk tolerance?

## Age Appropriate Investments

If you are close to retirement and you have all your money in a place of volatility, you should rethink your position. Common sense should jump up and bite you where it hurts. The average person (couple) has been saving for 25 to 35 years. The older you get, the more critical it becomes to protect your principal. You simply cannot replace losses that occur near to or during your retirement—certainly not after you have begun taking a stream of income. If you are under 45, you may have time to recover from significant losses. But if you are in your 50s, 60s or beyond, you will probably never recover from a sizable loss to your principal.

To avoid such losses, you should carefully choose the correct investments and financial tools today. You cannot fix at 85 what should have been done when you were 60. But whatever your age, problems need to be corrected now.

### Choosing What's Right for You

There should be a compelling reason for every investment that you purchase. Each position that you choose should fit you and your circumstances. For investments where your principal is at risk, there are reliable, independent, third-party sources from which you can gain the information that you need to help you make a well-thought-out and informed choice. You get to look inside, see the gears and the guts, and find out what makes them successful. Ask yourself: How will this benefit me? How does it work? What can I expect to gain from it? What is my exit strategy? Should you not want to do this for yourself—and most do not—the very least you should accept from a licensed *advisor* is full disclosure and transparency. A licensed advisor can generate side-by-side comparisons, showing where you are today and the improvements that are available to you.

## Gathering Information

Some of the items included in ***Your Retirement Workbook*** are as follows.

## Timing

- When will (did) you retire?
- "When can I afford to retire?" is one of the most common questions I receive. The correct answer to this question will deliver the minimum monthly income that you can rely on during your retirement. Then we get started on methods of growing this value.

## Lifestyle

- What are your biggest concerns?
- What are your priorities?
- What are your needs (short-term and long-term)?
- What are your goals (short-term and long-term)?
- Will you be moving or downsizing?

## Expenses

- Complete the spending plan worksheet. What are your expenses when working and when retired?

## Income

- How much income will you need? When will you need it?
- What are your pension choices? Do you have survivor benefits or replacement?
- What are your Social Security choices? (When optimizing Social Security benefits, a couple has hundreds of combinations from which to choose.)
- Do you have a Social Security replacement plan at the death of a spouse?

## Assets

- What are your current investments?
- What are your primary financial concerns?
- Are your current investments in line with your goals?

## Tax Planning

- You can choose from taxed, tax-deferred and tax-free investments.
- Learn how to efficiently get pre-tax money to an after-tax position.
- Take control of RMDs (Required Minimum Distributions).

- If you can control time, you can control taxes.

### Estate Planning

- Restricted beneficiaries
- Stretch IRA, keeping your inherited IRA tax-deferred
- Multi-generational planning
- Leaving a legacy
- Wills
- Trusts
- Durable Powers of Attorney
- Living Wills
- Special Needs

## Choosing Investments and Financial Tools

What blend of financial products will provide the best balance of growth, income and principal protection for you?

### Gaining Control Adds Confidence: Airplanes vs. Hot Air Balloons

My wife and I were sitting at home one day when our friends Terry and Nancy called. They said they wanted to come up for the weekend, and that they were going to take us flying. There was no other explanation offered—they wanted it to be a surprise. (I had previously flown Terry and his sons around in our Piper Cherokee.) Terry and Nancy showed up with a hot air balloon, which was neat. We rolled it out, filled it with air, heated the air and were off. As we drifted over neighborhoods, people emerged from their homes to view this strange aircraft. They looked like herds of mice from the air, trailing the balloon like a shadow. Our touchdown made the front page of the local paper, with a short article and a color photo. Later we were invited to other balloon events, including a week at the annual Balloon Fiesta in Albuquerque, New Mexico with more than 500 other balloons. All of this was enjoyable—traveling with the wind, quiet except for the noise of the burner and a crackling sound as it cooled. It was nice to get some "lighter than air" hours recorded in my pilot logbook. But as a fixed-wing pilot, there was always this nagging feeling of *lack of control.* Yes, you can go up and down slowly. But as for direction, you can only look and wish.

We all want control over our lives. Thus, we all want control over our retirement savings. This is the benefit of planning. ***Your Retirement Workbook*** is your opportunity to see the benefits of planning first-hand. You can find confidence here. Eliminating the unknown relieves anxiety and stress. Now is the time to start benefiting from newly discovered opportunities and avoid potential problems.

## Your Retirement Workbook

**Step 1.** In gathering information, the more accurate and complete the details, the better the results will be. Good data in, good plan out.

To make sure that you take all things into consideration download a copy of ***Your Retirement Workbook***. It is available for free download at:

www.WayneFisherFinancial.com

***Your Retirement Workbook*** includes the necessary forms for gathering your information in order to develop a retirement plan and to choose the investments and financial tools which will serve you best during your retirement.

**Step 2.** For information regarding a consultation, contact us at wayne@fisherfinancial.net or call (530) 243-2234 or (877) 594–4271.

# About the Author

Wayne Fisher moved his financial services business to Redding, CA in 1990 and later added a second office in Chico, CA. **Fisher Financial Tax and Insurance Solutions, Inc.** serves hundreds of clients throughout California and other states from Alaska to Virginia. Wayne has conducted financial seminars in libraries and restaurants for more than fifteen years, taught retirement planning courses in colleges and universities and hosted his own radio program for more than five years. He is a former underwriter for a property-casualty insurance company and managed a retail commercial insurance agency that provided business insurance in five states while living in East Texas. Wayne is a licensed fiduciary with a Security and Exchange Commission (SEC) Series 65 license.

Regardless of the direction the stock market and interest rates take in the future, you want a trusted advisor you can count on to provide you with straight, honest information and always look after your best interests.

FISHER FINANCIAL

TAX & Insurance

SOLUTIONS Inc.

# Copyright

**Surviving a Flawed System & Retiring with Confidence**



2400 Washington Avenue, Suite 120
Redding, CA 96011
(530) 243-2234

854 Manzanita Court, Suite 110
Chico, CA 95926
(530) 891-1117

www.FisherFinancial.net

ISBN-10: 1-946203-05-X
ISBN-13: 978-1-946203-05-2

Illustrations created by Jessica Fisher Burns, unless otherwise noted.

do not assume and hereby disclaim any liability to any party for any loss, damage, or disruption caused by errors or omissions, whether such errors or omissions result from negligence, accident, or any other cause.

Expert Press

www.ExpertPress.net